Strategies for Governing

STRATEGIES FOR GOVERNING

*Reinventing Public Administration
for a Dangerous Century*

ALASDAIR ROBERTS

CORNELL UNIVERSITY PRESS
ITHACA AND LONDON

Copyright © 2019 by Cornell University

All rights reserved. Except for brief quotations in a review, this book, or parts thereof, must not be reproduced in any form without permission in writing from the publisher. For information, address Cornell University Press, Sage House, 512 East State Street, Ithaca, New York 14850. Visit our website at cornellpress.cornell.edu.

First published 2019 by Cornell University Press

Library of Congress Cataloging-in-Publication Data

Names: Roberts, Alasdair (Alasdair Scott), author.
Title: Strategies for governing : reinventing public administration for a dangerous century / Alasdair Roberts.
Description: Ithaca : Cornell University Press, 2019. | Includes bibliographical references and index.
Identifiers: LCCN 2019011211 (print) | LCCN 2019012871 (ebook) | ISBN 9781501745607 (pdf) | ISBN 9781501745591 (epub/mobi) | ISBN 9781501714405 | ISBN 9781501714405 (cloth) | ISBN 9781501747113 (pbk.)
Subjects: LCSH: Public administration.
Classification: LCC JF1351 (ebook) | LCC JF1351 .R528 2019 (print) | DDC 351—dc23
LC record available at https://lccn.loc.gov/2019011211

> The idea of the state is the conscience of administration.
> —Woodrow Wilson, 1887

> The formation of states must be an experimental process.... Since conditions of action and of inquiry and knowledge are always changing, the experiment must always be retried; the State must always be rediscovered.
> —John Dewey, 1927

> The loss of the stable state means that our society and all of its processes are in continuing processes of transformation. We cannot expect new stable states that will endure even for our own lifetimes. We must learn to understand, guide, influence and manage these transformations.
> —Donald Schön, 1971

> Strategy should be thought of as glue that holds together the purposeful activities of state.
> —Colin S. Gray, 2015

Contents

Acknowledgments ix

Introduction: Time for a New Approach 1

PART I. KEY IDEAS

1. Summary of Propositions 23
2. Acknowledging the State 26
3. States and Societies 31
4. Leaders and Their Goals 35
5. Strategies for Governing 43
6. Factors and Forces 50
7. Laws, Organizations, Programs, and Practices 55

8. Aspects of Institutional Stewardship	59
9. Challenges in Strategy-Making	65
10. The Struggle for Mastery	72
11. Danger, Strategic Fragility, and Realism	77
12. Time and Progress	81
13. Unexceptionalism	87

PART II. DILEMMAS IN STRATEGY-MAKING

14. Efficiency or Extravagance	93
15. Tight or Loose Control	98
16. Separation or Connection	103
17. Present or Future	107
18. Commitment or Equivocation	112
19. Planning or Improvisation	116

PART III. APPLYING THE APPROACH

20. Research	123
21. Teaching	127
22. Practice	131
Conclusion: Grand Challenges	135
A Glossary of States	141
Further Reading	153
Notes	157
Index	193

Acknowledgments

This is my third book with Cornell University Press. It has been a pleasure to work with the press over the last ten years and, in particular, with my editor, Michael McGandy, whose thoughtful advice has made every book better. Thanks also to the anonymous reviewers of this manuscript and to colleagues who commented on early drafts and presentations.

This book is dedicated to my mother, Nancy Roberts, and my father, James Roberts, who passed away in 2018.

STRATEGIES FOR GOVERNING

Introduction

Time for a New Approach

This is a book about public administration and what its aims should be. It is intended for researchers in the field, practitioners in public service, and students preparing to become researchers or practitioners, but it will also interest readers concerned about building secure and thriving societies.

My argument is straightforward: In the United States, the field of public administration was launched almost a century ago by people with bold aspirations. They were not interested only in the efficiency of government offices; they wanted a thorough overhaul of the creaking American state so that it could manage the pressures of modern-day life. Unfortunately, this expansive view of the field's purpose has been lost. Over the last four decades in particular, the focus within the field has been mainly on smaller problems of management within the public sector. This narrowing of focus might have made sense in the United States and a few other advanced democracies in the waning decades of the twentieth century, but it does not make sense today. As we shall see, many people have recently protested this shrinking of ambitions. It is time for a change of direction. We need to recover an expansive view of the field, and I propose a way to do so.

I proceed from the premise that it is impossible to talk about public administration without also talking about the larger challenge of governing a state. Woodrow Wilson, often seen as a founder of American public administration, also made this claim in a famous 1887 essay. Before we can say how the state should be administered, Wilson insisted, we have to talk about the things that the state must do.[1] We can turn Wilson's proposition around as well: before we consider what the state ought to do, we must know what it is actually capable of doing. In other words, the overall approach to governing determines administrative priorities, while practicalities of administration constrain our choices about the overall approach to governing.

My argument has a sense of urgency as well. We must recover the capacity to talk about the fundamentals of government, because the fundamentals matter immensely. Right now, there are billions of people on this planet who suffer terribly because governments cannot perform basic functions properly. People live in fear because governments cannot protect their homes from war and crime. They live in poverty because governments cannot create the conditions for trade and commerce to thrive. They live in pain because governments cannot stop the spread of disease. And they live in ignorance because governments do not provide opportunities for education. The expectations that we hold of our leaders can be stated simply: They should protect us from foreign enemies, maintain internal order, increase prosperity, improve well-being, and provide justice. Even in the twenty-first century, most governments on this planet fail to do this.

In defense of leaders, it might be said that our expectations are easily stated but not so easily fulfilled. Governing is hard work. Leaders of most states struggle just to understand what is going on inside and outside their country's borders. Then they must determine the relative importance of national goals, given that resources are scarce and goals are often incompatible. Leaders must next decide, under conditions of great uncertainty, which policies are likely to achieve their priorities. Leaders struggle to execute these policies too. Institutions are hard to build and run effectively. It is not easy to find soldiers, bureaucrats, policemen, and judges who are competent and willing to follow instructions. And even well-considered plans go awry because of an unexpected change of circumstances.

The challenge of governing was described by the Florentine diplomat Niccolò Machiavelli a half millennium ago. Machiavelli warned the rulers of Italian city-states such as his native Florence that their work was fraught with danger. Sometimes the threat was posed by other city-states, and sometimes it arose within the city walls because people were restless and hard to please. A clever leader sought advice on how to build institutions that would bolster his authority both inside and outside the city walls. But even strong institutions could be toppled by the tempest of public affairs. They had to be renovated constantly to keep up with changing conditions, and this was very hard to do. States that did not constantly renew themselves, Machiavelli warned, were likely to collapse.[2]

Some commentators have suggested that Machiavelli lived in unusually precarious times. In some ways, though, the rulers of sixteenth-century Florence had it easy. Florence was merely a city-state: its walls contained only four square miles of territory and sixty thousand people. Today the average state has more than two hundred thousand square miles and more than thirty million people. Compared to Florence in 1500, China has a million times as much land and twenty-three thousand times as many people. The institutional apparatus required by a state like China is more vast and complex than anything Machiavelli could have imagined.

There are additional complications for today's rulers. Machiavelli warned about renewing institutions to keep up with the times, but the world in which he lived was relatively stable. In important ways, it was not much different when he died in 1527 than when he'd been born sixty years earlier. By comparison, the pace of change today—social, economic, technological—is blistering. The planet's current population of seven billion is also more restless: urbanized, literate, wired, and mobile. And they have higher expectations of their rulers. Standards for security and order, public services, and protection of human rights are more demanding today than they were in the sixteenth century.

The leaders of modern-day states have a difficult assignment. They must devise a strategy for leading their countries toward security, order, prosperity, and justice. Next, they must design and build institutions that translate their strategy into practice. And then they must deal with the vicissitudes of time and chance, adapting strategies and institutions in response to altered circumstances and unexpected events. To do this well, leaders need advice about the machinery of government—what it is capable of doing, how it should be designed and constructed, how it ought to be run, and how it can be disassembled and reconstructed. Researchers who work in the academic discipline of public administration should be expert in providing this sort of advice. One of their most important functions is helping leaders to devise strategies for governing that are effective, durable, and normatively defensible.

This was certainly the view of the people who founded the public administration field, even if they did not express it in exactly these words.

The Founders' Bold View of the Field

The academic discipline known as public administration is about one hundred years old in the United States. People sometimes say that it is older, pointing to Wilson's 1887 essay, but that is not quite right. The first self-styled school of public administration was established in 1922, and the first textbook in public administration, written by Leonard White of the University of Chicago, was published in 1926. Wilson's work did not get much attention until the 1930s, when professors of public administration invented a history for their new field, which included a contribution from a well-regarded then-recent president.

The first generation of scholars and practitioners in public administration were tied to a political movement in American politics known as progressivism, which coalesced in the 1890s and gained strength over the next two decades. American society was convulsed during these years by the emergence of big industries and cities, stark inequality and labor unrest, a surge in immigration, extraordinary technological advances, and shifts in the international balance of power. Americans had great hopes for their country. But many also worried that events could spiral out of control. Institutions designed for a simpler time did not seem sufficient for new realities. "The government of the part of the world in which we live," Luther Gulick warned, "is in many respects three generations behind our necessities."[3] Gulick was one of the leading figures in American public administration in the early twentieth century. He believed that progress required a complete reconstruction of the old order. The writer Walter Lippmann called this "the fitting of government to the facts of the modern world."[4]

The progressive movement faltered in the 1920s, as the United States enjoyed a moment of peace and prosperity. But it regained strength in the 1930s and 1940s as the global economy crashed, the European peace of 1919 collapsed, and the Cold War with the Soviet Union began. American democracy was tested severely in competition with fascist and communist rivals, and basic survival hinged on an overhaul of the "antique machinery" of American government.[5]

The discipline of public administration was invented to help with this overhaul. Academics in the new field defined their work broadly. They viewed themselves as architects of a renewed American state. Charles Merriam, another leader of the new field, summarized its main concerns crisply in 1944: "(1) external security, (2) internal order, (3) justice, (4) general welfare, and (5) freedom."[6] Researchers looked at the overall structure of the executive branch as well as the management of individual offices within it; military as well as civilian agencies; and legislatures and courts. They believed themselves to be engaged in a project "of continual creation, an unceasing invention of forms to meet constantly changing needs."[7] This project was thought to require a "historically conditioned sensitivity . . . an awareness of the ever-changing, inter-relating forces and factors comprising [a government's] environment and shaping its existence."[8] John Gaus described this as an "ecological approach" to research. Any scheme of government, Gaus insisted, had to account for "the elements of a place—soils, climate, location, for example—[and] the people who live there—their numbers and age and knowledge, and the ways . . . by which they get their living . . . [and] physical technology, social technology, wishes and ideas, catastrophe, and personality."[9]

The leaders of this new discipline were acutely aware of what would happen if government did not respond adequately to "the necessities of change."[10] The result would be economic and social chaos, subjugation to foreign powers, and the end of the great American experiment in self-rule. "The stakes are beyond price," Leonard White warned in the 1939 edition of his influential textbook on public administration, even before the outbreak of World War II. If democratic government failed in the United States, "an autocratic alternative may await the opportunity to seize power."[11]

Rise of the Public Management Approach

All that was eighty years ago. Several generations of scholars have worked in the field of public administration since then, and the boundaries and priorities of the field have changed significantly. For the last forty years, the tendency has been to focus more narrowly on problems of management within public agencies. This is sometimes called the "public management approach." There are associations and conferences exclusively dedicated to research on public management, leading journals that specialize in the field, and universities that offer degrees. Young scholars might be tempted to regard these institutions as permanent fixtures, but almost all of this apparatus has been built since the 1980s. And now the public management approach is so popular that it seems to have pushed public administration aside entirely.[12] "The discipline of public administration is in crisis," one observer lamented in the 1990s. "Courses and programs as well as whole institutes and schools are adapting, changing labels from 'public administration' to 'public management.'"[13] The trend has intensified since then.

The public management approach differs from classical public administration (as it is sometimes known) in important ways. It focuses mainly on the middle- or meso-level of government—agencies, agency networks, and programs. Its main concern is the ability of managers within agencies and programs to achieve objectives set by political overseers.[14] For example, one popular textbook describes public management as "the formal and informal processes of guiding human interaction toward public organizational objectives. The units of analysis are processes of interaction between managers and workers and the effects of management behavior on workers and work outcomes."[15] The emphasis is on efficiency—that is, on improving "the value for money achieved by public services," particularly in the delivery of education, healthcare, welfare, and other social services, as well as environmental protection and other forms of domestic regulation.[16] Less attention is paid to national security, diplomacy, and policing, and to the judicial and legislative branches of government.

Public management research has been dominated by scholars in the United States and a few other Western democracies, and this approach might make sense as a response to the distinctive social and economic conditions that prevailed in those countries after the 1970s. In the aftermath of World

War II, Western governments began providing more benefits to citizens, such as pensions, income support for the poor and disabled, healthcare, and subsidized college education. Many scholars called this the era of the *welfare state*. (The glossary defines this concept and other types of states mentioned later.) This was also the era of the *regulatory state*, as governments imposed more controls on economic and social affairs—for example, to limit pollution or prevent discrimination. The size and cost of government increased substantially, especially after the 1960s. More people paid income taxes than ever before.

By the 1970s, policymakers in Western governments began to see a backlash against big government. Many ambitious programs launched in the previous decade failed because their promoters had overestimated the difficulty of making them work or had misunderstood how the people would behave in response. The rate of economic growth also declined, and so did tax revenues, making it harder to pay for these new programs. Many citizens suffering because of the economic slowdown balked at higher taxes. Liberals who did not want to abandon these programs entirely had to find ways of repairing their defects and improving their efficiency. To survive the conservative assault, government had to "do more with less."[17] As Owen Hughes has observed, "governments were faced with declining real revenue [and] political demands to maintain services at the same levels. In these circumstances, the only avenue was to improve productivity."[18] This was the main problem that the public management approach was intended to solve.[19]

Ignoring the Big Picture

The public management approach was a rational response to the problems confronting leaders in a particular set of countries at a particular moment in history. But circumstances change, so that well-established ways of thinking about the world are no longer fit for the times. In recent years, the public management approach has been subject to assault from three directions.

Some criticism has come from scholars in the small number of developed countries that fostered the public management approach. A few complain about scholarly neglect of the security sector of government: national defense, intelligence and counterintelligence, and policing and counterterrorism.[20] This neglect is especially odd in the American context, given that most people in federal government work in the security sector. Some have even characterized the United States as a *national security state* or *garrison state*. Neglect of the security sector makes a little more sense in western Europe, where national defense does not have the importance that it did in the early twentieth century.[21] One explanation for this neglect may be that security functions were not immediately relevant to the crisis confronting western governments in the late twentieth century; social programs and regulation, not defense spending, were the lightning rods for public discontent. But conditions have changed in the last twenty years. We are now more focused on security problems: terrorism, the revival of tensions between great powers, failed interventions in Afghanistan and Iraq, and controversies over urban policing and the treatment of minorities. Public management research has had little to say about many of these problems.

The public management approach has also been criticized for its preoccupation with the meso-level of government. It has focused on agencies within government but not on the design and performance of government overall. The approach is said to have overlooked the "big questions" about public administration.[22] Brint Milward, one of the early advocates of public management, has criticized it for ignoring "basic questions about the capacity and purpose of the state."[23] Similarly, Robert Durant and David Rosenbloom have lamented the neglect of "'big questions' such as the political economy of administrative reform and its evolution over time."[24] "Big questions need to be addressed," another writer agrees, "to find new ways to govern peacefully, reduce tensions, and uncover solutions to the problems that bedevil societies in the fast-changing landscape of the twenty-first century."[25]

Other critics of public management warn that that researchers must attend to "the big picture," as Christopher Pollitt has called it: "the surrounding architecture of politics, economics, technology, demography and the natural environment which, however indirectly or slowly, pushes and shapes the actions of public authorities."[26] This big picture is constantly changing: there are "megatrends" or "large forces" that threaten to undermine social and economic well-being.[27] Pollitt emphasized three megatrends—technological change, climate change, and demographic change—but there are others as well.[28] Governmental capacities must be adapted to address the threats that emerge from such large-scale transformations. "The biggest challenge of governance," Donald Kettl has observed, "is adapting the institutions and processes of government to new problems it faces.... [This challenge] is ageless and universal."[29] In the short term, failure to adapt can lead to a decline in public trust of government, and in the long term, it might lead to a collapse of the state itself. "Nothing that gets out of sync with its environment lasts long," Kettl has warned. "That goes for governments just as much as dinosaurs."[30]

The fear of many scholars is that Western governments today are failing to adapt. This is sometimes expressed as a concern about the "dysfunctionality" of government in the face of new challenges.[31] Writers have warned about the ossification of the American government and the unsustainability of the American state as it is presently configured.[32] "Government at all levels," William Galston has written, "has become increasingly sclerotic and ever more misaligned with realities."[33] Francis Fukuyama has even suggested that the American state is decaying, a condition that arises when "institutions prove unable to adapt."[34] The collapse of trust in public institutions is taken as a symptom of this failure to adjust.[35]

Of course, this problem is not new. It is exactly the problem identified by scholars of public administration in the Progressive Era. As we have seen, those scholars attempted to address this problem by thinking broadly about the overall design of government and about the capacities needed within government to enable leaders to respond intelligently to changing circumstances. The complaint today is that the problem of adaptation is not regarded as a high priority within the field of public management. Indeed, it is not really identified as a problem at all. There is a substantial amount of research on organizational change *within* agencies or programs—again, research focused on the meso-level of government—but little on the adaptation of government as a whole.[36] The field does not take the long view, trying to identify long-term dynamics.[37] It responds to events rather than anticipating them.[38]

Western Parochialism

A certain bundle of institutional innovations became popular among Western leaders as they tried to make governments work better and cost less. Some sold off state-owned enterprises such as airlines or utility companies. Many hired private contractors to run prisons and schools and to provide other public services. Managers within government were "empowered" by loosening internal controls that had been adopted decades earlier to control corruption and patronage. Performance-measurement systems were introduced to create stronger incentives for public servants to perform well. Working conditions in the public sector were "normalized" to private-sector standards by weakening unions and other safeguards against maltreatment. Many public-sector workers were fired as government agencies were streamlined and right-sized. Governments adopted new information technologies to improve service and reduce staff.

This bundle of reforms was sometimes described as a "new paradigm" for public management, or simply as new public management (NPM).[39] Scholarly research of public management often focused on the implementation and assessment of NPM-style innovations. These reforms became so popular in the 1990s that people began to talk about a "global public management revolution" and a "global paradigm" for reforming government.[40] In 1999, Vice President Al Gore invited leaders from around the world to participate in a global forum on reinventing government, held at the State Department headquarters in Washington, DC. The purpose of the forum, according to Secretary of State Madeleine Albright, was to promote the "cause of efficiency and democracy . . . around the world."[41]

There was a strong impulse at the end of the twentieth century to emphasize how countries were converging on a single way of governing. The Soviet Union had collapsed only a few years earlier, and the model of a tightly planned economy had been discredited. Francis Fukuyama celebrated the "universalization of Western liberal democracy as the final form of human government."[42] Powerful organizations like the International Monetary Fund and the World Bank pushed poor countries to shrink government and expand free markets. Their reform formula came to be known as the Washington Consensus.[43] NPM and the Washington Consensus were tightly linked ideas: in a sense, NPM gave a more detailed plan of how an efficient, market-friendly government ought to be organized, and it seemed to be the one best way to run any country. Public management scholars helped to advance this view, perhaps unwittingly, by encouraging a global conversation on improving efficiency through NPM-style reforms.[44]

But many people were skeptical about this story of worldwide convergence. Even in the Western world, scholars questioned whether all governments were pursuing NPM-style reforms with equal enthusiasm.[45] And sharper criticism came from academics in non-Western countries. In east and southeast Asia, for example, scholars challenged the idea that the public management approach was applicable to their countries either as a framework for research or a program for reform. Some charged the public management movement with ethnocentrism and parochialism.[46] Asian academics pointed out that the journals and conferences that were focused on public management were dominated by researchers from a handful of wealthy, stable democracies in the West.[47] "The epistemic dominance of the western academic community," Shamsul Haque of the National University of Singapore observed in 2013, "is being increasingly questioned by critics with regard to the relevance and use of such knowledge in the Asian context."[48]

One way of questioning the relevance of the Western approach has been to highlight the distinctive needs of Asian societies. For example, Western leaders in the years after 1980 were preoccupied with reducing government intervention in mature economies. But many countries in east and southeast Asia were at a different stage of development in the 1980s and 1990s: they had poorer economies that seemed to need more guidance from government. They were inclined to follow the model of Japan—a *developmental state*—which became prosperous because of government planning, support to key industries, and protectionist trade policies.[49] Some Asian scholars accused the West of hypocrisy, because their countries were being discouraged from adopting interventionist policies that the West had relied upon in the nineteenth and early twentieth centuries.[50]

Leaders in south and southeast Asia also need to maintain public support, just as Western leaders do. But some Asian academics have a different view about how this need should be addressed. In the West, public anger has been interpreted as a response to the rapid growth of the public sector. Citizens seem to be frustrated by out-of-control spending and regulation.[51] Consequently, the goal has been to restore trust by making government leaner and more disciplined. However, circumstances are different in several Asian countries. In some, there simply is no general crisis of legitimacy: in India and China, for example, large majorities express support for government.[52] And where distrust is a problem, it might be the result of too little government rather than too much. In this context, the goal is to bolster trust by expanding the supply of basic services such as policing, transportation, water and sewage, electricity, education, and healthcare.[53]

In some Asian countries, attitudes about the need for a traditional civil service differ as well. In the West, the drive for austerity often meant abandoning the old ideal of the civil service as a high-status, lifelong vocation.[54] Some Western governments even began recruiting private-sector executives directly into top-level public-sector jobs. (The United Kingdom hired a television executive to run its prison service.) In some Asian nations, however, the national civil service plays an important role in unifying diverse peoples and bolstering the authority of central government.[55] Dismantling the civil service in this context seems unnecessary and even dangerous. Similarly, reducing internal controls within the civil service might make sense in the West, where problems of corruption and nepotism have abated over decades, but not necessarily in some Asian countries, where the need for such controls is still clear.[56]

Rather than stressing the distinctive needs of their countries, some Asian critics have emphasized the mismatch between Western-style reforms and socioeconomic conditions. For example, Tobin Im and Alfred Tat-Kei Ho have warned that imported reforms "are often not compatible with the inherent political, social, and cultural institutions" of non-Western countries.[57] Similarly, Gerald Caiden and Pachampet Sundaram have counseled reformers to take stock of the "shifting combination of history, culture, politics, economics, sociology, ideology and values in each country."[58] Other scholars have emphasized the importance of "unique country-specific contextual factors . . . [such as] political history, party politics, macroeconomic considerations, state tradition . . . and the state of civil society."[59] Western-style reform may also be stymied by the absence of supporting institutions, such as a robust rule-of-law system, that are taken for granted in the West.[60]

A third way of critiquing Western-style public management reforms is to emphasize their incompatibility with the way that leaders in Asian countries think about national strategies. From this point of view, it is not needs or conditions themselves that matter; what really matters is the leaders' perception of those needs and conditions, their judgment about the most critical national objectives, and the plans they have formulated to pursue those objectives. As Anthony Cheung puts it, reform is "mediated by . . . the strategies of the governing elites" in East Asia.[61] Cheung emphasizes that the renovation of administrative systems is just one part of a larger plan for addressing political and economic problems, and he says Western management reforms will be imported and properly implemented only if they fit with that larger plan.[62] Similarly, Tobin Im observes that imported reforms have succeeded in South Korea only when they were consistent with the "governing philosophy" of leaders.⁶³ And in China, according to Lan Xue and Kaibin Zhong, "the vision and judgment of the political leadership is crucial" in determining whether imported reforms will be implemented.⁶⁴

One way or another, many Asian scholars are arguing that the public management approach simply does not fit the realities of governance in their countries. And we can see that the Asian critique of the public management approach parallels the critique made by commentators in the West itself. Asian scholars who call attention to distinctive needs, conditions, or governing philosophies are insisting that it is impossible to think about management reforms without attending in some way to "big questions" and the "big picture," to use the vocabulary of Western scholars. The overarching concern in Asia is the renovation of government to meet the requirements of societies that are evolving rapidly. Conversation around this question requires an explicit acknowledgement of the fundamental objectives of government—such as maintaining national cohesion, promoting growth, and improving the well-being of citizens—as well as a broad understanding of national conditions. The public management approach does not encourage this sort of high-level analysis.⁶⁵

Scholars in the East and West are essentially making the same critique of the public management approach: both camps suggest the need to recover the broad approach of public administration scholars from the first half of the twentieth century—an approach that deliberately examines the aims of state action and the ways a state must be designed to further those aims, in a particular place and moment in history.

Neglect of Fragile States

There is a third camp of researchers who, rather than criticizing the public management approach, have mainly ignored it. These researchers are focused on improving governance in *fragile states*. This term came into scholarly usage in the 1990s, referring to countries whose governments "have weak capacity to carry out basic functions of governing a population and its territory" and whose claim to authority may be actively resisted by powerful groups within society.⁶⁶ (In practice, the division between stable and fragile states is almost the same as that between developed and developing countries.⁶⁷) The aim of reformers in fragile states is to build the fundamentals of governmental capacity and legitimacy. The public management approach has little to say about this, largely because these fundamentals are taken for granted in the developed West.

The project that must be undertaken in fragile states is sometimes referred to as peacebuilding or statebuilding. One of its basic goals is to establish order within national borders, which requires the development of police and security forces that can be relied on to follow commands and use force responsibly. Legislatures must also be established to adopt laws that are regarded as legitimate by powerful societal factions. Then independent courts must be set up to apply those laws fairly. In addition, fragile states lack bureaucracies capable of providing essential services. Governments also need the capacity to monitor and control basic aspects of economic activity, such as cross-border trade, and they must build a sense of common identity and loyalty within the population.[68]

Academic interest in statebuilding coalesced in the 1990s, driven by a desire to reestablish order in war-torn countries in Africa, Asia, and Eastern Europe following the collapse of the Soviet Union. It was given impetus in the early 2000s as the United States tried to rebuild states that were identified as bases for terrorism. (In other words, statebuilding is also an instrument of American foreign policy.) The field of inquiry is now well-established. Graduate degrees and research centers dedicated to peacebuilding and statebuilding have been launched, and a vast amount of scholarly material has been produced.[69] The scholarly community works in concert with a network of national development agencies, international organizations, and non-governmental organizations that support projects to improve public institutions in struggling countries.[70]

Clearly, this enterprise is engaged with public administration problems, but it is entirely disconnected from the academic community that specializes in public management. Statebuilders are interested in aspects of government that seem to be well-established in Western democracies and are consequently overlooked by Western scholars. There may be problems of weakening trust in some Western countries, but none are afflicted with armed rebellions. By and large, leaders in the West can rely on the loyalty of their people. Internal peace and order has been achieved: there are no "ungoverned spaces" within the national borders of Western states. Institutions for making and enforcing laws are also consolidated, and governments are able to monitor economic activity and collect taxes. The public management approach can focus on middle-level problems such as efficiency and effectiveness precisely because all this infrastructure already exists. Public managers in developed countries may safely assume that they will have money to spend, that employees will put their professional obligations ahead of tribal loyalties, that workers will not be killed when they visit field offices, and that agency orders will be enforced by the courts. Bureaucrats in fragile states do not take any of this for granted.

In other words, the public management approach has yet another blind spot: it is not good at thinking about the problems of fragile states. If there were only a few fragile states in the world, this might not be a significant defect. But several nongovernmental organizations have developed measures of state fragility, all of which show that fragility, not stability, is the prevailing condition in most of the world.[71] The Fund for Peace has found that only 54 of the 178 states included in its Fragile States Index can be regarded as stable. The rest suffer from some degree of fragility. Sixty-six of these fragile states were judged to be at severe risk for social, economic, and political turmoil,[72] and nine of the ten most populous countries are fragile according to this index. Overall, there are more people living in fragile states than there are in developed countries like the United States.[73] And even developed countries may not be safe: in 2017, the Fund for Peace perceived a worrisome decline in social and political cohesion in the United States and other advanced democracies.[74]

The way of thinking that prevails in statebuilding literature would be appreciated by Western and Asian critics of the public management approach and by Progressive Era scholars in public administration. That literature focuses on big questions. By necessity, it is concerned with identifying functions essential to state survival.[75] The literature is also attentive to the big picture; that is, the ways in possibilities for governmental reform are constrained by "historical, political, and economic specificities."[76] And above all, statebuilding literature is suffused with an awareness of danger; the risks and costs of state failure are fully appreciated. Western scholars used to think this way too. As Leonard White said in 1939, "The stakes are beyond price." White and his colleagues did not talk about "fragile states," but they understood the concept. A state that cannot perform essential functions "is sick," Charles Merriam warned in 1945, "perhaps unto death."[77] This was the malady that the field of public administration was invented to remedy.

Need for a Macro-Level Approach

The public management approach was invented in response to a crisis of governance in a handful of affluent, stable Western democracies in the waning years of the twentieth century. An attempt was then made to use the approach as a template for research and practice around the world. But challenges of governance have mutated in Western democracies, making the public management approach no longer entirely fit for those countries. The template has proved to have limited usefulness for most other countries as well, largely because their leaders face different challenges and have different ideas about how to move their countries forward.

We are left, therefore, with a problem. If we continue to rely on the public management approach, we will overlook critical questions about governance in the twenty-first century. We need a new approach for thinking about public administration that accommodates new conditions in Western democracies and enables a global conversation in which the circumstances of non-Western states are given appropriate attention. We need to recover the capacity to do the sort of work that American scholars in public administration had in mind when they launched the enterprise almost a century ago. My aim is to show how we might do this.

To be clear, I am not arguing for abandonment of the public management approach. Rather, my purpose is to complement this approach with another that is more suited to looking at big questions and the big picture. We can make an analogy to other scholarly disciplines. In the field of economics, there is a generally accepted distinction between research on bigger questions about the national economy (macroeconomics) and research on smaller questions about the activity of firms and households (microeconomics). In political science, scholars make a similar distinction between high-level research on political regimes and more grounded research on the political behavior of individuals. In the study of history, meanwhile, a distinction is made between research on the long-term development of social structures and the short-term unfolding of events. We could go on. Many scholarly fields recognize the need for tools that allow them to address big questions as well as small questions about human activity. However, public administration lacks a comparable facility. We have refined our ability to engage in meso-level

Table 1 Levels of analysis in public administration

Macro-level	Study of the governance strategies that are devised by leaders to advance critical national interests and the ways in which these strategies influence the overall architecture of the state.
Meso-level	Study of the design, consolidation, administration, and reform of specific institutions–that is, laws, organizations, programs and practices–within the state.
Micro-level	Study of the attitudes and behavior of officials within the state apparatus and of people who are subject to their authority.[1]

[1] I have modified the definition commonly used by proponents of behavioral public administration, which refers to the attitudes and behavior of "citizens, employees and managers." There are many more ways of categorizing people inside and outside the state apparatus.

research, but we lack—or rather, have abandoned—the capacity to engage in macro-level research.

I have already noted many scholars in the East and West who share the belief that we need to move beyond meso-level research by working at a higher level of analysis.[78] But there are scholars of public administration arguing for research at a lower level of analysis as well. They propose a "behavioral approach to public administration" that takes a "micro-level perspective" on the behavior of citizens, employees, and managers within the public sector. "By micro-level," Stephan Grimmelikhuijsen, Sebastian Jilke, Asmus Leth Olsen, and Lars Tummers have explained, "we mean that the unit of analysis focuses on psychological processes within or between individuals."[79] It is important to emphasize that there is no tension between calls for micro- and macro-level research.[80] A well-developed field should acknowledge three distinct levels of analysis—micro, meso, and macro—and have the capacity to pursue rigorous scholarship at each level (see Table 1).[81]

In this book, I assemble a conceptual toolkit for engaging in macro-level research within the field of public administration. At the center of the proposed approach is a concern with the invention and execution of *strategies for governing*. I will give a brief sketch of the approach here. We begin, as did most early scholars in public administration, by recognizing the state as the main building block of political order in the modern world. States have leaders, and leaders are concerned with a limited set of goals. Leaders develop opinions about the relative importance of these goals and the best ways to achieve them, given their perception of their countries' circumstances. In other words, they invent a strategy for governing that incorporates judgments about priorities and tactics. Next, leaders design and build institutions to implement these strategies. Leaders operate in a world of great uncertainty and turbulence, and they often realize that strategies are misguided or have become outmoded. Consequently, strategies and institutions must be renovated continually.

The world of practice is never as neat and orderly as the preceding paragraph might imply, however. There are many constraints, including variations in the competence of leaders, that make it tremendously difficult to formulate coherent strategies and put them into operation. I examine these constraints throughout this book, especially in chapters 9 through 11. Perhaps it would be better to say that all leaders struggle to behave strategically. Even the least competent of leaders has some ideas about priorities and methods, which are the essential elements of strategy. Similarly, there is a limit to what leaders can do by themselves: all must rely on institutions to give expression to their strategies.

All of this institutional groundwork—designing, building, consolidating, administering, renovating—falls squarely within the domain of public administration. Leaders choose strategies for governing, but their choices must be informed by advice about the architecture of government: how it ought to be designed and what load it can carry. Scholars in public administration should be skilled in providing this advice.

In the following chapters, I elaborate on the concepts and propositions that are essential to this new approach. It may seem odd to lay out these concepts and propositions so directly. One of the conceits of much contemporary research in public administration is that we are ruthlessly empirical: we simply describe the world as it is rather than imposing notions of how it ought to be. Flatly asserting concepts and propositions, as I appear to do here, seems decidedly unempirical. But there is no difference between my approach and that taken by advocates of public management research forty years ago. They, too, began by flatly asserting a new way of viewing the world of public administration.[82] To assemble their conceptual toolkit, they often appropriated ideas from other disciplines that suited their needs.[83] That is, they engaged in an exercise of intellectual bricolage. And at first, they were often criticized for fuzzy theorizing. However, there was no way around this criticism. Eventually, public management scholars would generate a substantial body of methodologically rigorous research. But the unavoidable and messy first step was to describe the metes and bounds of the territory they wished to explore and to gather tools that seemed useful for exploration.

We must repeat this exercise today. The conceptual apparatus built in the 1980s was useful in addressing the main challenges of that era, which were associated with the crisis of the welfare and regulatory state. However, new challenges require new tools. In some ways, I simply recover ideas that were familiar to the first generation of scholars in public administration. I also borrow ideas from other disciplines—law, political science, sociology, and history—in which scholars address similar questions. Sometimes I have adapted and simplified those ideas so that they are better suited to our requirements. At a few points, I also introduce new ideas to mortar together those that have been revived, borrowed, and adapted. I do not make an exhaustive review of all the scholarly literature that might be connected to the proposed approach. That would be an impossible task, and the final product would be indigestible. Thus, the goal pursued in part 1 is to give a broad overview of a new approach.

A theme throughout this book is the difficulty of crafting governance strategies that are effective, durable, and normatively defensible. In part 2, I experiment with a few essays on the challenges that confront leaders as they invent and execute strategies. I do not provide neat solutions for these challenges, because there are no such solutions; rather, there are only messy and temporary responses to prevailing conditions. Similarly, part 3 briefly considers how this new approach will affect the way we think about research, teaching, and practice in public administration. This question also arose forty years ago: inventing the public management approach meant overhauling programs of research, graduate courses, and understandings about how practitioners should approach their daily work.[84] Again, my observations are not intended to be definitive. Rather, the purpose is to suggest the direction in which our conversation might proceed.

In summary, this is a preliminary work. Undoubtedly it contains conceptual errors, false starts, and tangents. The same was true of scholarship in public management at its beginning forty years ago. It will take time to refine ideas, eliminate digressions, and prove the usefulness of the framework. Still, the imperfections in this book should not distract us from the larger point: The field of public administration has narrowed its ambitions in the last four decades; it has surrendered too many important questions to scholars in other disciplines; and it must find some way of recovering its former aspirations. The approach outlined here may be helpful in doing this.

PART I

Key Ideas

Chapter 1

Summary of Propositions

This is a summary of propositions that are emphasized within the proposed macro-level approach to public administration. These propositions are examined in the following chapters.

1. Today, and for the foreseeable future, the fundamental unit of political organization is the state.
2. Every state is a constituent of an international system of states.
3. Every state asserts the exclusive authority to regulate life within a defined territory.
4. Every state has leaders; that is, a relatively small group of people who have substantial influence over the ordering of state goals and the means by which those goals are pursued.
5. Generally, leaders try to
    a. maintain and improve their own positions within the state apparatus;
    b. increase power and legitimacy within the state system;

c. increase power and legitimacy within the state's own territory; and
   d. increase national prosperity.
6. In addition, leaders ought to advance human rights for the population that is subject to their authority.
7. Conversely, leaders may construe as threats or problems any developments that jeopardize the pursuit of the above goals.
8. The behavior of leaders is guided by governance strategies that describe priorities—that is, the ordering of goals—and the means by which those priorities will be pursued.
9. In general, these aspects of the governing environment must be taken into account as leaders set priorities and decide how those priorities will be pursued:
   a. The distribution of power within the state system.
   b. The composition, distribution, and movement of the governed population.
   c. Patterns of economic activity.
   d. The geography and climate of the governed territory.
   e. The inventory of social and physical technologies.
10. Leaders implement governance strategies by designing, consolidating, administering, and renovating institutions—that is, laws, organizations, programs, and practices. Every state consists of a complex of institutions that expresses a strategy for governing.
11. Crafting and implementing governance strategies is difficult for these reasons:
   a. Goals are not always compatible, so advancing one goal sometimes means compromising another.
   b. There is uncertainty about which policies are most likely to advance goals.
   c. The existing body of institutions, laws, and practices must be accommodated.
   d. The environment for which the strategy is designed is turbulent, so priorities and methods frequently need to be reconsidered.
   e. The analytic capacity of leaders and executive agencies is strained by the complexity of strategy-making.

12. Governance strategies are varied, fragile, and ephemeral. They are designed to accommodate specific conditions, and they must be adjusted frequently as conditions change. This means that institutions, laws, and practices must also be renovated frequently.
13. There is an unavoidable conflict between the need to consolidate institutions, laws, and practices, and the need to preserve adaptability.
14. The proper timeframe for studying the evolution of governance strategies and the institutions, laws, and practices that express such strategies is at least generational. Shorter timeframes create an illusion of robustness and stability.
15. The U.S. experience in crafting and implementing governance strategies is not exceptional.
16. Scholars and practitioners in the field of public administration should be experts in the overall design, construction, administration, and renovation of those institutions that constitute a state. They should use this expertise to help leaders craft governing strategies that are effective, durable, and normatively defensible.

Chapter 2

Acknowledging the State

The following chapters explore some of the concepts and propositions that should be central to a macro-level approach to public administration. The first step is to acknowledge the fundamental unit of political organization in the modern world: the state.

In several scholarly disciplines, the importance of the state is taken for granted. Many political scientists regard the state as "the natural container of politics."[1] No concept, say Colin Hay and Michael Lister, "is more central to political discourse and political analysis."[2] Similarly, the sociologist Anthony Giddens calls the state "the pre-eminent power-container of the modern era."[3] Specialists in international relations regard the state as "the primary unit of political aggregation in world affairs"[4]; political geographers regard it as "the basic building block of the world political map";[5] and international lawyers regard it as the "primary unit of political and economic organization."[6]

And yet the concept of the state is largely omitted from conversation in public administration, the field most directly concerned with the translation of political aspirations into governmental action. This was not always so. Up until the early 1950s, scholars in public administration routinely talked about the state. In an 1887 essay that is now regarded as a "founding manifesto" for the new field, Woodrow Wilson said that the concept of the state was "the conscience of administration." Any "science of administration," Wilson insisted, had to be connected to a theory about the appropriate role of the state.[7] Public administration, Marshall Dimock agreed in 1937, was simply "the state in action."[8] But this way of thinking fell out of fashion decades ago. Today, entire textbooks in public administration are produced without reference to the concept of the state. The field operates without acknowledging that the United States is a state that is also part of a community of states or that a main concern of American policymakers is executing tasks essential to state survival. In American public administration, the state is the ghost in the text: it is always there, but its presence is not recognized.

What is a state? Many have attempted definitions. Max Weber famously described the state as "a human community that successfully claims the monopoly of the legitimate use of physical force within a given territory."[9] This definition is imperfect. States never achieve a complete monopoly on the use of force within a given territory. It is enough to gain "effective control," in the argot of international law. Indeed, states may hobble along even when their hold over much of their territory is tenuous. (These are sometimes called *fragile states*.) Weber's reference to the "legitimate" use of force also creates difficulties. If we put that aside for the moment, it would leave us with a hard bottom line: that a prerequisite for existence as a state is the capacity of authorities to suppress rivals for power within well-defined borders. This is roughly accurate, although it could be argued that survival as a state also depends on the accomplishment of tasks other than the attainment of effective control (chapter 5).

Another approach to creating a definition emphasizes the composition of a state in addition to the tasks that it must perform. For example, John Hall and John Ikenberry defined the state as "a set of institutions" that maintain authority within a territory.[10] Hall later joined with John Campbell to provide a more extensive explanation:

> In the most generic and ahistorical terms, the state is a set of institutions designed to maintain order in a given territory and protect its population from other states.... The institutions of states typically include decision-making

bodies (e.g., councils, senates, parliaments, tribunals), defense and security apparatuses (e.g., armies, navies, militias, national guards), and a set of laws and enforcement mechanisms (e.g., police, councils of elders, judiciary)—all of which are to some extent in the hands of an elite set of rulers and their staff.[11]

Other scholars have offered similar definitions. Some describe the state as a complex or ensemble of institutions that jointly exercise supreme authority within a territory.[12] S. E. Finer described the state as "an organ served by specialized personnel" such as "a civil service to carry out decisions and a military service to back these by force where necessary."[13] Theda Skocpol has defined the state as "a set of administrative, policing, and military organizations headed, and more or less well coordinated by, an executive authority."[14]

This approach to a definition, which emphasizes the way in which the state is constituted, could be modified in two ways. Institutions consist of people who fill roles and execute routines. It is a friendly amendment, therefore, to define the state not just as an institutional complex that performs certain tasks but also as the group of people who populate those institutions and share responsibility for those tasks. Similarly, people must have a shared understanding of what those institutions are trying to do and how they are supposed to work. The substance of the state consists not just of institutions and people but also these shared understandings.

The state has another critical aspect: it possesses a status or standing referred to as *statehood*. The conferral of this status is the final and critical step in transforming an institutional complex into a state. Not only must an institutional complex wield authority as a matter of fact; its right to exercise authority must also be recognized by other actors. The most critical form of recognition comes from other states and is guided by principles of international law. An institutional complex that wins this sort of recognition—and thus becomes a state in the eyes of the international community—is less likely to be attacked, is free to engage in diplomacy with other states, and is entitled to join international organizations. At the same time, the authority of this institutional complex needs to be accepted by the governed population. This is usually what we mean when we talk about *legitimacy*, the word used by Weber.[15] People within a territory must acknowledge that an institutional complex has the right to rule. There are practical reasons why this is so. States cannot govern through the use of force alone.[16] Leaders depend on "habitual obedience of the bulk of the population."[17] Samuel Finer once suggested that cultivating such obedience is "the principal art of government."[18]

It is helpful to distinguish the concept of the state from three other concepts. First, there is a difference between state and government, and especially central government. In the United States, for example, the central government is certainly an important part of the institutional complex that constitutes the state—but that complex also includes fifty state governments, forty thousand local governments, and fifty thousand special-purpose governments.[19] In addition, there are private organizations—such as political parties and contractors—that play a key role in governance as well as international organizations through which American leaders advance their interests abroad. These should also be counted as components of the state apparatus, if only on the periphery. Moreover, as I have noted, this whole apparatus must accomplish certain things before it can be counted as a state—such as effective control over territory and the attainment of standing.

An important question is how this institutional complex ought to be designed so that it is durable and competent in performing essential tasks. This is a query about the overall architecture of the state. The field of public administration, comprised of experts in the design and renovation of institutions, ought to have something to say in answer to this question. The substance of that answer hinges on our judgment about top-priority tasks and about what institutions can and cannot do. As I will explain later, these judgments relate to the overall strategy for governing.

A second conceptual distinction should be drawn between states and *nation-states*, even though these terms are often used interchangeably. A nation-state is formed when most of the governed population shares a language, culture, and history, and so constitutes a distinct nation. For many years it was asserted that a state could not survive unless its population constituted a single nation, and for this reason, political leaders often pursued policies to increase linguistic and cultural homogeneity.[20] Frequently, minority rights were abused in the drive for conformity. Conversely, it was often asserted that a population constituting a distinct nation should be allowed to form its own state. This was the principle of national self-determination, which still motivates secessionist movements in many countries. However, many states have endured though their populations comprise two or more distinct nationalities. Leaders have found ways to grant autonomy to population subsets that form distinct nationalities without completely breaking up the state. By doing this, they have established *multinational states*.

Also, there is no necessary connection between the concept of the state and statism. Statist philosophies are those that encourage extensive regulation of economy and society, and give priority to the collective interest (as expressed by central institutions) rather than to individual rights. Statists sometimes have a romantic notion of the State (typically capitalized in this usage) as a manifestation of the general will of the people, assuming that there is such a thing. But scholars who talk about the state are not necessarily committed to statism. On the contrary, many states are designed to avoid statism by dividing and constraining the power of public institutions. This is the formula pursued by liberal democracies, especially those that have divided power between two or three tiers of government. Liberal democracies are still states, even though they are built on anti-statist principles.

Chapter 3

STATES AND SOCIETIES

There are roughly 195 states in the world today. It is impossible to give a more precise number, because leaders disagree about whether some states should be recognized. For example, South Korea does not recognize North Korea, and vice versa. Several countries refuse to recognize Israel. Israel does not recognize Palestine, mainland China does not recognize Taiwan, Serbia does not recognize Kosovo, and so on. Still, 195 is a good working figure. The United States recognizes 194 other states, while 193 states have been granted membership in the United Nations. Most of the world's territory is now claimed by states. The average state governs six hundred thousand square kilometers of land and thirty million people.

As a matter of international law, every state is independent, or sovereign, within its territory. Broadly, this means that the leaders of a state are free to manage their internal affairs however they wish. This principle is not as clear-cut as it once was, because states are increasingly willing to intervene when other states abuse their citizens or pose a threat to international security.[1] Still, the basic idea is that "all states are equal: each has the right not to be dictated to by the others."[2] It is a "fundamental axiom" of international law that each state has exclusive power over its territory.[3]

Of course, law and practice are different things. There are many ways in which states can pressure each other to change behavior. And the authority of states is often challenged, sometimes violently, by the governed population. To varying degrees, all states are vulnerable to attack from without and within. This reality was expressed by Niccolò Machiavelli in 1513 when he wrote about the city-states of renaissance Italy and particularly about his home city Florence. "A prince must have two fears," Machiavelli wrote: "one internal, based on his subjects; the other external, based on foreign powers."[4]

Another way to think about Machiavelli's statement is to consider the position of a state in relation to two forms of society. First, every state is a member of the global society of states, also referred to as the system of states.[5] This system is about four hundred years old and has evolved considerably in that time. The system began with the division of Western Europe into a small number of major states, each with formal independence, in the seventeenth century. The Peace of Westphalia, a series of treaties that ended the Thirty Years' War, is usually viewed as the moment in which the European state system was born. It was transformed into a global system—a true "world of states"—by the collapse of European empires after World War II. Most of the states that exist today were established after that war. The last substantial burst of state creation was triggered by the collapse of the last European empire, the Soviet Union, in 1991.

The world of states is sometimes described as an anarchy.[6] There is no supreme power that has the capacity to impose order and regulate conflicts among states. Every state must be on guard against attacks on its territory and people. States jostle for control over disputed territories, access to critical resources (such as water and oil) and foreign markets, and the support of other governments. Competition between states is unrelenting. Herbert Butterfield observed that states live in a "situation of Hobbesian fear."[7] Every state tries to achieve security by increasing its power within the state system but never fully succeeds, precisely because all other states are doing the same. This predicament is known as the "security dilemma."

This picture of brutal competition can be overdrawn. The international system has an architecture that has been constructed to moderate its worst effects. Major states maintain diplomatic services and a network of embassies that allow constant communication with other states. This diplomatic capability is a critical part of the institutional complex that constitutes a state, because no state can exist unless it has the capacity to communicate with other states. In fact, the first executive agency created by the U.S. Congress under the Constitution of 1788 was the Department of Foreign Affairs, now the Department of State. There is also a well-established body of international law and convention that provides a structure for dialogue among states. International law provides the criteria for deciding whether an aspiring state should be admitted to the society of states, protects ambassadors and embassies, and provides a protocol for inter-state communications. States are bound together by a dense web of bilateral and multilateral treaties and by membership in dozens of international organizations, the most prominent of which is the United Nations. The launching and conduct of war is also regulated by international law. In the end, powerful states can flout international law and ignore international organizations, but they pay a price in terms of reputation and influence. The force of international law is demonstrated by the effort that states make to justify their conduct even when rules are bent or ignored.

The international system is not rigid, and it need not be organized as a community of formally independent states. In medieval Europe, the political order was much more confused. Power was divided among a welter of principalities, duchies and baronies, and city-states, many of which were linked by dynastic, military, and commercial alliances, all of which were nominally subject to the authority of the Western Christian church.[8] Only a century ago, the system would have been more accurately described as a mix of *empires* and non-imperial states. And as I have noted, the superstructure of international law and organizations is more extensive today than it was in 1945. In the 1990s, some scholars even speculated that the era of the independent state was over because of the growing power of international organizations and movements. Events of the last fifteen years have put an end to this speculation. The world order is likely to remain structured as a society of formally independent states for the foreseeable future.

A second state-society relationship that must be recognized is the relationship between the state and the population living within the territory claimed by that state. This relationship has sometimes been viewed as one in which the state looms over the territory and wields absolute authority over the population. (See the etching that serves as the frontispiece for Hobbes' *Leviathan*.) In this view, the domination of society by the state is emphasized. This view reflects the aspirations of some early statebuilders rather than the way the world really worked, either then or now.

The reality of governance is flatter and more equivocal. The state consists of a set of people who assert power over their compatriots. But people do not want to be controlled and are inclined to resist subordination; hence the "internal fear" of rulers described by Machiavelli in 1513. But the difficulties described by Machiavelli, the factionalism and intrigue of the Florentine city-state, seem trivial today. At that time, Florence had a population of about sixty thousand people. There are twice as many people living in the city of Springfield, Massachusetts today. The current population of the United States rivals that of the entire planet in 1513.[9]

Leaders may obtain the compliance of reluctant subjects in several ways: by appealing to shared ideals, offering physical safety and prosperity, promising to share power or exercise restraint in the use of power, and by punishing disobedience. Every state uses some combination of these techniques. The choice of techniques has implications for the architecture of the state: appropriate institutions must be built before techniques can be applied. But no combination of techniques is wholly and permanently effective. Even the most stable states experience periodic crises of legitimacy—moments when a specific formula for achieving legitimacy has exhausted its usefulness and needs to be revised. Indeed, it has been argued that the United States is experiencing such a crisis today. In democracies, crises of legitimacy may result in leaders being thrown out of office through elections. Authorities can also be challenged through mass protests, political assassinations and terror attacks, secessionist movements and rebellions, and coups. We sometimes imagine that these forms of resistance do not happen in the developed world, but in reality, all of these types of crises have occurred in one Western country or another since World War II.

Chapter 4

Leaders and Their Goals

Within every state is a group of people who have a large degree of control over the way state power is exercised.[1] They directly influence decisions about how goals are prioritized and pursued and ways in which institutions are constructed or renovated so that these decisions can be realized. These are the people who need advice on macro-level questions of public administration—that is, on big questions relating to the architecture of the state.

What should we call this group of people? The answer seems straightforward when we talk about non-democratic states: we call them rulers. Look at a few news stories:

> Even authoritarian governments want to frame major political events with a sense that the state of the union is strong, so it's no surprise that China's rulers are trying to juice the economy ahead of the Communist Party's approaching five-yearly congress. —*Bloomberg News*, August 8, 2017

> Russia's rulers are convinced that smart intelligence work did play a major role in the collapse of the Soviet Union. And, of course, thoughts of a payback did enter their minds more than once. —*Newsweek*, January 15, 2017
>
> Ever since Kim Jong-un took over as the young, untested ruler of North Korea seven years ago, he has promised his country a future free from deprivation. —*New York Times*, May 26, 2018

In the United States, however, the answer to this question has changed over time. Before World War II, Americans often used the term *ruler*, as shown in the following examples:

> Whatever the form of government, it can only persist by consent of the governed. That consent can be won or retained only when the rulers meet the demand of their citizenry. —*San Diego Union*, August 24, 1930
>
> It may not be true that any boy can become president, but it is true that any bright boy may become one of America's rulers. For the highest authority in America is the supreme court, and its nine members represent every class and faith that is typical of our nation. —*Rockford Register-Republic*, May 18, 1936
>
> Only our own rulers can get us into war! They are the ones for us to watch and to worry over. —*Richmond Times Dispatch*, April 29, 1939

After World War II, however, use of this term faded in the United States. Ordinary people talked about leaders, and social scientists introduced even more anodyne terms: *policymakers* and *decisionmakers*. Words like these were less jarring in a democratic age. They obscured the fact that people were being ruled and that the people in charge wielded a "monopoly of force." But this effacement of power was misleading, as Woodrow Wilson had acknowledged decades earlier:

> The authority of governors, directly or indirectly, rests in all cases ultimately on force.... Happily there are in our own day many governments, and those among the most prominent, which seldom coerce their subjects, seeming in their tranquil noiseless operations to run themselves. They in a sense operate without the exercise of force. But there is force behind them nonetheless because it never shows itself. The strongest birds flap their wings the least.[2]

Or as Mahatma Gandhi observed more succinctly: "no ordinary government can get along without the use of force."³

We can call the people in charge either *leaders* or *rulers*, as long as we are clear that there is no meaningful difference between the two terms. These are the people who wield the power of the state. We can and should make judgments about the appropriate form of rule—about the ways that leaders should be selected and the constraints that should be imposed on their use of power—but that is a separate matter.

The identification of leaders in a large, federalized liberal democracy is not straightforward. (Nor is it as easy as we are inclined to believe in nondemocratic states like Russia and China; we underestimate the complexity of those systems.) Clearly the president is a leader of the American state and so are key members of Congress. Political appointees and career bureaucrats also count as leaders if they exercise substantial influence over the content of overall strategy. Lower-level public servants usually do not exercise enough discretion to be counted as leaders. The *Rockford Register-Republic* might have been right in counting Supreme Court justices as leaders, although perhaps not judges in lower federal courts. Governors and legislators in major states might also be counted. There is a limit to how precise we can be. We are interested in the "pivotal positions" and "strategic command posts" within the institutional complex that constitutes the state; or in other words, in the small number of personnel who "exert active power" over the setting of national priorities and the means by which they will be pursued.⁴ Moreover, we are interested in the way that these leaders think about their work. This has been called the "official mind": the composite of "beliefs about morals and politics, about the duties of government, the ordering of society and international relations" that are shared by leaders.⁵

It is also possible to describe, in general terms, the set of goals that leaders pursue. Indeed, it was once taken for granted that the study of public administration was impossible without identifying these goals. "Organization and social purpose cannot be disassociated," the public administration scholar Marshall Dimock wrote in 1951. "Every question of organization is a matter of policy or of politics and involves the ends of the state."⁶ In his influential 1939 textbook, Leonard White observed that courses in public administration needed to give "adequate attention to the nature of society, to the ends of the state. . . . The ends of administration are the ultimate ends of the state itself."⁷ White even enumerated those ends: "the maintenance of peace and order, instruction of the young, equalization of opportunity, protection against disease and insecurity, [and] adjustment and compromise of conflicting groups and interests."⁸ White's colleague Charles Merriam offered another formulation of the "ends of government" in 1944: "(1) external security, (2) internal order, (3) justice, (4) general welfare, and (5) freedom." Any state that failed to accomplish these goals, Merriam said, was "sick . . . perhaps unto death."⁹

The practice of defining the "ends of the state" fell out of fashion in public administration but has recently been revived in other quarters. Since the late 1990s a new scholarly field known as statebuilding has emerged, with the aim of giving advice about the design and consolidation of public institutions in war-torn and fragile states. In fact, statebuilding is a kind of scholarship in public administration, adapted to the realities of governance outside the developed world. Experts working in this new field are explicit about state goals, just as American scholars were three generations ago. One influential text identifies ten essential "functions of the state," ranging from the establishment of public order to the protection of individual rights.¹⁰

In crafting a list of goals for state leaders, we are obliged to think both as realists and idealists. As realists, we acknowledge some goals that leaders will be motivated to pursue out of self-interest or by force of circumstance. For example, it seems likely that leaders will try to maintain, and if possible to improve, their own position within the state apparatus. This assumption is a staple of analysis in political science:

> Survival in office is . . . the essence of politics. The desire to survive motivates the selection of policies and the allocation of benefits; it shapes the selection of political institutions and the objectives of foreign policy; it influences the very evolution of political life. We take as axiomatic that everyone in a position of authority wants to keep that authority and that it is the maneuvering to do so that is central to politics in any type of regime. . . . All actions taken by political leaders are intended by them to be compatible with their desire to retain power.¹¹

We can question whether this ought to be a primary goal of state policy, and we will see that it also conflicts with other goals. But there is little doubt that survival in office should be counted within the set of likely goals.

A second goal is to increase the power and legitimacy of state institutions within the territory claimed by the state. To a point, this is a matter of necessity, a prerequisite for existence as a state. As I have already observed, one of the prerequisites for statehood, as a matter of international law, is effective control of territory.[12] To put it another way, states must have the capacity to resist challenges to their authority. Of course, effective control—the establishment of civil peace—is a minimal requirement. States constantly try to improve knowledge about their territory and its population and to refine their ability to regulate the behavior of people and nature.[13] And as I have noted, the capacity to shape the behavior of a large population through force alone is limited. At some point, people must be persuaded that complying with directives is the right or prudent thing to do. Cultivating popular legitimacy is therefore an important part of extending control over territory. There are many ways to cultivate legitimacy: stoking fear about disorder or nationalist pride, offering guarantees about the rule of law or elections, devolving power to lower tiers of government, or simply bestowing money and services.[14]

A third goal is the extension of power and legitimacy within the state system. As in domestic affairs, leaders seek to improve their knowledge about the lay of the land—that is, they gather intelligence about the motivations of other states and the threats that they pose. And they try to build up military capacity and economic clout so they can defend territory, forge alliances, and assure access to critical resources and markets. Legitimacy within the state system is mainly expressed through recognition by other states; that is, by formal admission into the community of states. A less tangible form of interstate legitimacy is captured in the concept of "soft power"—the capacity of one state to obtain the cooperation of other states through the appeal of its policies and way of life rather than through coercion or payment.[15]

A fourth goal is the increase of national prosperity. Prosperity helps leaders in several ways. Prosperous societies are easier to govern: citizens are happier, factional tensions are less intense, and any popular discontent or factional conflict can be reduced through largesse from the state. A larger economy also means more tax revenue to pay for diplomats, soldiers, police, and other public services, assuming that the capacity to extract taxes is well established. At the same time, prosperity increases influence within the society of states. Leaders are in a better position to recruit allies by providing aid, while other states have a stronger motivation to cooperate in exchange for access to markets.

A fifth possible goal for leaders is the advancement of human rights.[16] To some degree, this is also a matter of prudence for leaders. Increasingly, membership in the society of states is affected by internal policies regarding human rights: states that abuse their people badly might be excluded from international organizations and even attacked by other states. A reputation for cruelty also undermines legitimacy at home and soft power within the society of states.

But prudence is a weak guarantor of human rights: it may discourage outright abuses but not much more. When we talk about the advancement of human rights, we are mainly talking about a goal that leaders *ought* to pursue, regardless of their inclinations. Indeed, a clear conflict of goals is immediately clear. The Universal Declaration of Human Rights says:

> The will of the people shall be the basis of the authority of government; this will shall be expressed in periodic and genuine elections which shall be by universal and equal suffrage and shall be held by secret vote or by equivalent free voting procedures.[17]

Obviously, leaders cannot respect this command without compromising their ambition to survive in office. Leaders in the United States and other democracies have struggled with this tension for decades. Almost universally, they have acknowledged that their hold on office is constrained by their capacity to continue to win elections.

So far I have described the goals of leaders in positive terms, as a striving *toward* certain things, such as tenure in office, security and power at home or abroad, prosperity, and advancement of human rights. These goals can also be expressed in negative terms. Leaders are often caught off guard by events that jeopardize their tenure in office, national security, economic growth, and human rights. In other words, they must anticipate and respond to threats as well as pursue opportunities. However, this does not make the calculus for leaders any simpler: avoiding one threat may mean aggravating another. For example, applying strict measures in response to security threats could threaten civil liberties or economic growth.

Statecraft is the art of sorting out how authority should be exercised from day to day while also building and renovating those institutions through which authority must be exercised. As I will show in the following chapters, it is difficult work, and not simply because of conflicts among goals. Leaders also wrestle with pervasive uncertainty, rapidly changing circumstances, and weaknesses within the institutions that they rely on to execute their plans.

Over time, leaders have developed a distinctive way of thinking about all these complications. This way of thinking is focused on the advancement of critical national interests, and it includes assumptions about the kind of evidence required for decision-making, a set of techniques for dealing with analytic challenges such as uncertainty and goal conflict, and rules of thumb about the handling of recurring problems. Historically, the term used to identify this distinctive way of thinking is *raison d'état*, or the reason of state. "Reason of state," said the sixteenth-century philosopher Giovanni Botero, "is the knowledge of the means by which [a state] may be founded, preserved and extended."[18]

The concept of *raison d'état* originated in an era of dynastic government and chronic disorder, which may explain why its early exponents seemed so ruthless and indifferent to conventional morality. In that more brutal time the priority was survival, and *raison d'état* was laser-focused on that goal.[19] This specific mentality is particularly offensive today. But this does not mean that the concept of *raison d'état* is obsolete. Even now, there is a way of thinking that is peculiar to the leadership of states, adjusted to fit modern understandings about democracy, human rights, and international law, among other things.[20] For example, when experts in statebuilding describe techniques for managing the "internal contradictions, difficult trade-offs and dilemmas" that arise in fragile states, they are delineating an updated form of *raison d'état*.[21] So are scholars in development studies who search for ways of "being explicit about trade-offs and priorities . . . in a world in which all good things cannot be pursued at once."[22]

This challenge of wrestling with contradictions and uncertainties is not limited to fragile or poor states. Consider these comments from President Barack Obama as he discussed U.S. policy on climate change shortly before the signing of the Paris Accord in 2015:

> When we get to Paris at the end of this year, we're now in a position for the first time to have all countries recognize their responsibilities to tackle the problem, and to have a meaningful set of targets as well as the financing required to help poor countries adapt. And if we're able to do that by the end of this year . . . then we will at least have put together the framework, the architecture to move in concert over the next decade in a serious way. But

having said all that, the science keeps on telling us we're just not acting fast enough. My attitude, though, is that if we get the structure right, then we can turn the dials as there's additional public education, not just in the United States but across the world, and people feel a greater urgency about it and there's more political will to act.... So the science doesn't change. The urgency doesn't change. But part of my job is to figure out what's my fastest way to get from point A to point B—what's the best way for us to get to a point where we've got a clean-energy economy. And somebody who is not involved in politics may say, "Well, the shortest line between two points is just a straight line; let's just go straight to it." Well, unfortunately, in a democracy, I may have to zig and zag occasionally, and take into account very real concerns and interests.[23]

Here we see a leader working through complex questions of priority-setting and institutional design, wrestling with the tension between what ought to be done and what can be done, and struggling with the entanglement of foreign and domestic politics. Skill and specialized knowledge are required to do all of this well. This is what we mean by *raison d'état*. Macro-level scholarship in public administration is concerned with improving *raison d'état*, inasmuch as it connects the high-level ambitions of leaders with a knowledge of what institutions are capable of doing and how institutions can be built, run, and renovated.

Chapter 5

STRATEGIES FOR GOVERNING

Leaders develop an overall view about how state authority ought to be exercised, which I call their strategy for governing. This strategy includes an understanding about national priorities—that is, the ordering of goals—and also about methods of pursuing those priorities. The institutional apparatus that constitutes a state is the means by which strategy is put into place. It is the expression of strategy. Experts in public administration provide advice on how to build or renovate institutions so that they align with overall strategy. They also warn leaders against strategies that rely on untenable assumptions about building, running, and renovating institutions. And these experts make judgments about the morality of strategies that they help to design and execute.

Leaders within a state often have differing views about the best strategy for governing. Frequently, though, there is agreement on fundamentals. Within the United States, for example, there is rarely disagreement on basic principles such as federalized government, the separation of powers, free elections for key positions, and the constitutional protection of basic rights. Most American leaders also accept the desirability of free market capitalism, the need for a powerful military apparatus, and leadership in international diplomacy. There are arguments about the application of principles—What is the right balance of power between the executive and legislative branches? How rigorously should industry be regulated?—but not about the principles themselves. No one calls for the establishment of a unitary state, authoritarian rule, state ownership of all major industries, or unilateral disarmament. This overall formula—which in the 1930s and 1940s came to be known the "American way of life"—is generally accepted as the best way of preserving security, prosperity, and freedom.[1]

Sometimes an even deeper agreement about strategy may emerge. In the 1980s, for example, Republican politicians led by President Ronald Reagan pushed for a particular interpretation of basic principles: they urged economic deregulation, freer trade, lower taxes, reduced spending on social programs, and a shift of power to the states, among other things. This program was called Reaganism. This was a label for a specific strategy for governing. By the late 1990s, many Democratic politicians, including President Bill Clinton, had conceded the battle over these policies. It became possible to talk about a Reagan-Clinton consensus on important aspects of domestic and foreign policy—that is, about the core elements of a new strategy for governing.[2]

Many American leaders thought other countries should adopt this governance strategy as well. As noted in the introduction, some experts referred to the Reagan-Clinton formula as the "Washington Consensus" on how to run a country.[3] In 2002, President George W. Bush said that the basic components of the American approach—free enterprise, democracy, and freedom—were the "single sustainable model for national success."[4] In other words, Bush was asserting the emergence of a single, universally applicable strategy for governing. Within the scholarly field of public management, a similar opinion was sometimes advanced: that the world was experiencing a "grand, global isomorphism of governmental structures and practices."[5]

However, the experience of the last two decades has given ample reason to question this notion of global convergence. Chinese leaders, for example, are not moving toward the liberal-democratic model. On the contrary, they are refining a distinct strategy for governing.[6] The "China model," as it has been called, rejects separation of powers, federalization, free elections, and individual rights, on the premise that these policies will undermine governmental effectiveness and social stability. In China, the Communist Party supervises personnel in key positions throughout the bureaucracy. Limited experiments with free market policies have contributed to rapid growth, but critical financial and industrial enterprises are still state-owned. Government-controlled media celebrate the recovery of national honor following China's humiliation by Western powers in the nineteenth century. Chinese leaders are convinced of the superiority of this governance strategy over that of Western-style liberal democracy. Surveys suggest that an overwhelming majority of Chinese people—indeed, a much larger share of the population than in most advanced democracies—are satisfied with their country's direction.[7]

Russian leaders also reject the notion that there can be a "uniform, standardized model" of governance.[8] Russian leaders believe that U.S.-style policies would undermine its social stability, already weakened by the collapse of the Soviet system in the early 1990s. The Russian governance strategy of 2018—sometimes called Putinism—shares some of the features of the China model, such as strict control of media and cultivation of national pride. But it also has important differences. For example, democracy is "managed" and not rejected entirely. There is no strong party apparatus as in China, and grand corruption often serves as a glue that holds political and corporate elites together. Russian leaders rely heavily on their control over gas and oil exports to strong-arm neighboring states. Russian foreign policy is also aggressive and militaristic, in contrast to the policy of "quiet rise" that has been pursued by China. Russian leaders persist with this overall strategy because they believe it is most likely to advance critical foreign and domestic goals, given the "special circumstances" in which the country finds itself.[9]

Russian leaders are not alone in believing that special circumstances influence how their country should be governed. Most leaders think they face unusual conditions. And even when leaders face roughly comparable conditions, they may have different ideas about how to handle conflicting goals or uncertainties about tactics. As a result, we should expect tremendous diversity in the content of governance strategies. This does not always involve an outright repudiation of ideals like the rule of law, democracy, and individual rights. Even within the community of liberal democracies, for example, there is a wide variation in how these ideals are put into practice.

Governance strategies also vary substantially over time, as leaders adjust to changing circumstances. The "American way of life" described by writers in the 1930s did not include the military-industrial complex that was built up after 1941 or adequate protection for the civil rights of African Americans. And attitudes about the role of government in the United States changed again after the election of 1980, as I have noted. Similarly, the "China model" that prevailed in 2019—sometimes given the label "Xi Jinping Thought"—differed substantially from the "China model" of 1970, which relied on Soviet-style planning of the economy, and even from the "China model" of the early 2000s.[10] Mao Zedong, China's supreme leader until his death in 1976, would be shocked by the tolerance his successors have shown for free markets and private wealth. Russia's governance strategy has also changed radically since 1970: not only has Russia abandoned state planning; it has ceased to exercise suzerainty over many neighboring states.

The wide variety of strategies that leaders can pursue is indicated by the common scholarly practice of developing typologies of states. Scholars have identified *fiscal-military states*, *night-watchmen states*, *welfare states*, *administrative states*, *garrison states*, *developmental states*, *petro-states*, and dozens more, as the glossary shows. All of this scholarly inventiveness constitutes an effort to impose some order on the extraordinary variety of forms that states have taken over the past five hundred years. But categorization has its limits. The categories we create are always too simplistic: any governance strategy has many dimensions, not just the one or two that can be captured in a label. (Is the United States a welfare state, a regulatory state, an administrative state, or a national security state? Yes.) There is also a temptation to turn categories into ideal types, with the result that we pose questions from the wrong point of view. Rather than asking positively what strategy leaders appear to be pursuing, we ask why they are *not* pursuing some idealized strategy; hence, the extensive literature that considers why the United States is a "welfare state laggard." And the project of categorization makes us insensitive to the fragile, ephemeral character of governance strategies. Circumstances change quickly, and so do state strategies. If we insist on describing a state as type X, we must add the caveat: *for the moment.*

Recognizing that governance strategies are tailored to special circumstances does not mean that all have the same moral weight. For example, we ought to question strategies that neglect human rights. In addition, we can ask whether strategies are likely to be effective on their own terms; that is, in achieving the goals that have been identified as priorities by leaders. And we can ask whether they are likely to be durable—whether they will stand up over the long run. But any judgments that we might make about the morality, effectiveness, or durability of particular strategies cannot be made in the abstract. They must take account of the conditions that confront leaders at the time the strategy is formulated.

In sum, the leaders of all states invent strategies that describe national priorities and lines of action for achieving those priorities. Strategies for governing are not necessarily contained in formal plans, and they are not always fully articulated.[11] Often, large parts of a governance strategy are not put into words: they are simply taken for granted, as part of the generally accepted approach for dealing with certain problems. But even the most inexpressive leaders are compelled by events to make decisions and thus to convey through action their predispositions about priorities and methods. Strategy can be inferred from a pattern of behavior.[12]

The concept of a "strategy for governing" is related to the concept of "grand strategy," which has been deployed in the field of international relations and security studies for decades.[13] The concept of grand strategy was introduced in the nineteenth century to describe an overall policy regarding the use of armed forces in war. The intention was to distinguish between "the large, broad plan for winning a whole war on several fronts . . . [and] the localized strategy of the commander of a single army."[14] The era of total war (1914–1945) led military thinkers to expand the concept. In 1941, B. H. Liddell Hart defined grand strategy as a "national war-policy" that explains how all the resources of a nation—military, economic, and political—will be applied to achieve war aims.[15] Soon afterward, Edward Mead Earle defined grand strategy in similar terms, as "the art of controlling and utilizing the resources of a nation . . . to the end that its vital interests shall be effectively promoted against enemies."[16]

The notion of grand strategy was revived in the 1980s by two historians at Yale University, Paul Kennedy and John Lewis Gaddis.[17] Kennedy said that grand strategy was concerned with the "husbanding of national resources" so that a state could survive in "an anarchic and often threatening international order." This project, he said, had to be pursued in peacetime as well as wartime.[18] Gaddis agreed, insisting that "the management of states . . . [demands] the calculation of relationships between means and large ends" over long stretches of time.[19] Gaddis, like Kennedy, still tied grand strategy mainly to the goal of national security.[20]

However, other American scholars have advanced definitions of grand strategy that seem to broaden the range of possible goals beyond national security, to include other aspects of foreign and even domestic affairs. Hal Brand, for example, is less definite about the ends of grand strategy: he has defined it simply as "the intellectual architecture that gives form and structure to foreign policy . . . [and provides] a purposeful and coherent set of ideas about what a nation seeks to accomplish in the world, and how it should go about doing so."[21] Edward Luttwak has observed that strategy may be oriented toward a wide range of goals:

> [Some] seek power over other states, or even territorial expansion; others desire only to keep what external power and influence they have, while focusing on domestic goals, including the increase of prosperity; some governments are active on the world scene primarily to claim economic aid in various forms . . . and some others seek external support precisely to be left alone by their enemies.[22]

Similarly, Peter Trubowitz has recently argued that grand strategy, "the broadest level of foreign policy," can be focused on many objectives: security, power, wealth, national honor, and even the leaders' own hold on executive power.[23]

The concept of grand strategy has expanded about as far as it can without bursting through the walls of international relations and security studies. First applied to describe the overall deployment of armed forces, it was extended to include the application of non-military resources toward war aims, then to the pursuit of security in peacetime as well as wartime, and then to the pursuit of multiple goals besides strictly-defined national security. The only significant barrier that remains is the insistence that grand strategy is concerned with the domain of foreign policy alone. But this is an arbitrary line to draw: it is a distinction that is important to professors but irrelevant to leaders. Leaders do not have one grand strategy for managing foreign affairs and another for managing internal affairs—and if they did, neither one could properly be called a grand strategy. The true grand strategy would be one level higher.

The arbitrariness of a division between foreign and domestic affairs is increasingly recognized, although we have hesitated to take the final step in abandoning it. Students of international relations now acknowledge the extent to which foreign policy is driven by "domestic considerations."[24] And students of American government acknowledge how the design of domestic institutions and policies is influenced by "international factors."[25] The entanglement of foreign and domestic affairs has always been clear to leaders of smaller and more vulnerable states. In sum, neither aspect of policy—foreign or domestic—can be designed or understood on its own. Everything must be made to fit together, and the label we can give to this overall scheme is the strategy for governing.

Chapter 6

Factors and Forces

The architecture of the state—the overall design of its institutions—is guided by the prevailing strategy for governing. The formulation of this strategy requires judgments about the relative importance of state goals and the methods by which those goals will be pursued. These judgments are not made solely through abstract reasoning. Decisions about priorities are also based on an assessment of threats and opportunities that are perceived within a particular set of circumstances. Similarly, decisions about methods of governing hinge on perceptions of what is feasible in those circumstances. I could put this another way and say that governance strategies must be adapted to prevailing conditions as they are perceived by leaders.

This way of thinking about public administration is not new. Granted, the scholars who founded public administration in the first half of the twentieth century did not talk explicitly about strategies for governing. They were more likely to talk about the "ends of government" and the design of "administrative systems." The words used to describe circumstances also varied. Scholars talked about environmental factors, external forces, contextual conditions, societal imperatives, and many comparable concepts.[1] There was no standardization of vocabulary.

Still, there was general agreement on the proposition that the architecture of government had to be appreciated as a response to broader circumstances. Luther Gulick insisted in 1948 that "administrative developments, like organic developments," could not be understood without regard to "the compulsions of the environment in which they exist."[2] "To understand an administrative system," Lynton Caldwell agreed in 1955, "requires an awareness of the ever-changing, interrelating forces and factors comprising its environment and shaping its experience."[3] The study of public administration, Robert Dahl wrote in 1947, must account for "the varying historical, sociological, economic, and other conditioning factors that give public administration its peculiar stamp in each country."[4]

Some scholars elaborated on this basic idea. John Gaus of the University of Wisconsin proposed an "ecological approach" to the study of public administration that would explain how the aims and forms of government action were "coerced" by changes in the environment. Gaus enumerated the "environmental factors" that might be considered:

> People, place, physical technology, social technology, wishes and ideas, catastrophe, and personality.... An ecological approach builds, quite literally from the ground up; from the elements of a place—soils, climate, location, for example—to the people who live there—their numbers and ages and knowledge, and the ways of physical and social technology by which from the place and in relationships with one another, they get their living.[5]

Leonard White of the University of Chicago also subscribed to the ecological approach. All "systems of administration," White wrote in the 1939 edition of his textbook on public administration, are deeply affected by "contending forces" in their environment, including geographic, climatic, economic, and technological influences.[6] White later developed this theme in an award-winning series of books about the evolution of American government, published between 1948 and 1958.[7] American leaders, White observed in these books, were often "coerced by events" and "frustrated by circumstances." The federal administrative system, he said, had evolved in response to an array of "external forces," such as great power rivalries, internal conflicts, economic developments, and technological innovations.[8]

Writers of that period alternated discussion between *factors* and *forces*, as though the two words described the same idea. But the terms are not strictly interchangeable. The concept of social forces was invoked frequently by American political scientists, sociologists, and historians in the first decades of the twentieth century. Their ambition was not just to describe the world around them; they wanted to say something more troubling. The language of social forces conveyed the notion that society was moved by currents that were deep, swift-moving, poorly understood, and treacherous. Often, social forces were said to be blind and powerful.[9] The capacity of government to control these forces was cast in doubt. The concept of environmental factors, by contrast, carried none of these implications. It did not convey the same fear about the adaptive capacity of governments. Of course, anxieties about how to master the "great unconscious forces of American life"[10] were justified at that time as they are today. Still, that question can be separated from the simpler proposition that "administrative systems" are shaped by "environmental factors."

The first generation of scholars in public administration identified several factors that typically influence governance strategies. The first two are aspects of nature: geography and climate. For example, geography determines the vulnerability of a state to attack by other states as well as the manner in which that state must be defended. Until the advent of long-range bombers and intercontinental ballistic missiles, the United States appeared to be protected by oceans and consequently spent little on its army, except during the Civil War. The expanse and contours of land and water also influences the capacity of a state to assert control within its borders, and it shapes decisions about centralization or decentralization of governmental authority.[11] Similarly, the ability of states to stoke economic growth or exercise influence abroad hinges on their endowment of natural resources. Climate also affects prospects for economic growth as well as patterns of disease and susceptibility to extreme weather events.

A second factor is the profile of the population within the territory controlled by the state. The population might be described in many ways: by settlement and migration patterns; age or education; healthfulness and patterns of morbidity; and the presence of sections or factions—racial, ethnic, religious, linguistic, economic, or ideological. Of course, this is a very large set of potential considerations. It might be helpful to put it this way: a fundamental concern of a state is its capacity to maintain control over people within a territory. How this goal is achieved hinges on the characteristics of the people and the land they inhabit.

A third factor is the structure of the economy. By this, I mean patterns of production, trade, consumption, and finance. Economies differ in the extent to which activity is structured through markets, the extent to which markets are formalized, and the extent to which those markets are rigid or dynamic. Some economies rely heavily on the extraction and processing of natural resources, while others specialize in manufacturing, services, or finance. Economies also vary in the extent and type of interconnection with other national economies. All of these considerations affect the content of state policy profoundly. They influence the capacity of government to extract taxes, mobilize for war, wield influence over other states, redistribute income and wealth internally, and promote long-term growth.

A fourth factor is the inventory of available technologies, including physical technologies such as those used to capture, distribute, and convert energy. (In the last century, this has consisted primarily of fossil fuel extraction, refining and distribution, and combustion.) Physical technologies also include ways of communicating and transporting people, materials, and weaponry. In addition, there are social technologies, or organizational know-how, relating mainly to methods of coordinating large numbers of people, either through bureaucracies, networks, or markets. The capacity of states to wield authority at home or abroad hinges on the availability of such technologies to states and their rivals, internal and external. Indeed, competition between states has been a powerful incentive for the development and diffusion of new technologies. Of course, technological sophistication also shapes prospects for economic development.

A final factor is the distribution of power within the society of states. When international conditions are truly anarchic—when there is no dominant power to impose order—states are also more likely to invest heavily in national defense and diplomacy. The same is true when neighboring states are powerful enough to challenge a claim to territory. And when a state acquires the status of a superpower—as the United States did after World War II—the architecture of the state apparatus changes dramatically. A superpower learns how to sustain military complexes that span the globe. It also invests more in the construction of international institutions and concentrates more power in the hands of executives in central government.

All these factors were familiar to early scholars in public administration. The major events of era—the Great War of 1914–1918 and the World War of 1939–1945, the "great pandemics" of influenza and polio in the period between the wars, the Great Migration from the South to the North, the Great Flood of 1927, the Great Drought of the 1930s, the Great Depression, and the advent of an extraordinary battery of new technologies—vividly showed their importance. These events compelled a redefinition of understandings about the role of government in American life—in other words, a wholesale revision of the strategy for governing. And this revision, in turn, required the wholesale renovation of the institutional complex that constituted the American state. In fact, the field of public administration was invented to support this strategic reconfiguration.

Chapter 7

Laws, Organizations, Programs, and Practices

As I noted earlier, many scholars define the state as a set or complex of institutions that are established to perform certain functions. We can hone this definition. States have leaders whose behavior is guided by strategies that define priorities and methods for pursuing those priorities. Institutions are built and renovated to implement such strategies; they are the "tools of the trade of statecraft."[1] The result of such construction and renovation is an institutional complex that expresses a strategy and also constitutes the state.

One immediate objection is that this institutional complex is built up over decades and even centuries, and that it seems unreasonable to describe it as simply an expression of the strategy preferred by the current generation of leaders. This criticism is fair. The state might be more accurately described as an accretion or composition of institutions that have been established at different points in time in an effort to implement a succession of governance strategies. Most of this complex is taken for granted by leaders. It expresses the prevailing understanding about goals and methods, much of which is tacitly accepted by today's leaders. Leaders usually adjust prevailing strategies rather than attempting a root-and-branch overhaul. They concentrate their rhetoric and labor on those parts of the institutional complex where there is a serious mismatch between existing arrangements and their preferred strategy.

Much scholarly effort has been invested in the definition of *institution*. Some definitions are quite abstract. Samuel Huntington defined institutions as "stable, valued, recurring patterns of behavior."[2] James March and Johan Olsen described them as "collections of interrelated rules and routines that define appropriate actions in terms of relations between roles and situations."[3] Douglass North has said that institutions are "the humanly devised constraints that shape human interaction."[4] And James Mahoney and Kathleen Thelen have called them the "relatively enduring features of political and social life that structure behavior and that cannot be changed easily or instantaneously."[5] There is nothing wrong with such definitions, but as one scholar has observed, they might be "a little too general to be terribly helpful."[6]

Four particular kinds of institutions are of interest when we discuss the architecture of the state. The first are laws. These are general rules of conduct that dictate how people and organizations inside and outside of the state should behave. One variant is constitutional or basic law, which provides the framework for the operation of the state. Another variant is statute law, which typically consists of rules generated by legislative assemblies. A third variant is subordinate legislation, which usually consists of regulations or rules made by executives and bureaucrats under authority granted by statutes. This typology is not exhaustive, but it accounts for the main forms of law found in today's states.

Organizations make up the second form of institution that is critical to the architecture of modern states. By organizations, I mean agencies, departments, offices, bureaus, and so on—groups of people who are organized for the purpose of executing specific tasks. Often, organizations exercise authority granted by law; these groups are sometimes referred to as formal organizations, precisely because they are established by law.[7]

Organizations are responsible for implementing programs, a third important type of institution in the modern era. The program is a familiar concept in public management and budgeting. The U.S. Government Accountability Office defines a program as "an organized set of activities directed toward a common purpose or goal that an agency undertakes or proposes to carry out its responsibilities."[8] A large department within the U.S.

government may be responsible for dozens and even hundreds of programs, depending on how the concept is defined.

Some scholars might say that I am taking a "formal-legal" approach to the study of institutions because I have focused on appearances, the "organized and evident institutions of government," the laws that ostensibly regulate conduct, and the apparatus through which power is supposed to be exercised.[9] In the mid-twentieth century, many American political scientists firmly rejected this way of thinking about government, insisting that it was necessary to study the ways government *really* worked. Sometimes, these scholars suggested, leaders simply ignore the law and formal structures: formal-legal arrangements are merely window dressing, set up with the intention of deceiving observers about the true character of a regime. An extreme illustration is provided by Paul Johnson, as he described how the Soviet state operated under Stalin:

> By the mid-1930s, Stalin . . . had made himself an autocrat *de facto* though not *de jure*. In theory, as party general secretary, his powers were strictly limited, by the politburo, the Central Committee, and the party itself, especially when meeting in congress. All the various constitutions make this perfectly clear. But the constitutions were nugatory. So far as the exercise of power at the top was concerned, they existed only on paper. By 1934 Stalin had extended the practical power of the secretariat to overrule any other body.[10]

A similar criticism has been made against Russian president Vladimir Putin: that he props up a "facade of democracy," which disguises the actuality of centralized and arbitrary rule.

In fact, criticisms of formal legalism in the 1950s and 1960s were overwrought. Students of politics have always recognized that there is a gap between appearances and realities. In the eighteenth century, for example, British and American radicals insisted that constitutional forms obscured the reality of government by conspiracy and corruption.[11] A century later, Walter Bagehot distinguished between the "dignified" and "efficient" parts of the British constitution: between the "old and rather venerable" rules about how government was supposed to operate and the new and unacknowledged mechanisms (such as the cabinet system) that made the enterprise work.[12] The American Frank Goodnow, writing at the supposed zenith of formal legalism, said that his 1900 book on government was intended to show how "the formal governmental system as set forth in the law is not always the same as the actual system."[13]

We continue to recognize the gap between formalities and actualities in Western states today. We work with the understanding that "governing arrangements . . . are not quite what they seem."[14] There are informal practices that are so firmly established that they can be counted as institutions, according to the general definition of that concept offered by Huntington and others, even though these practices may not be recognized in law and may even be inconsistent with law. This gap is not always a sign that leaders are operating with bad intentions. Sometimes, leaders are just engaging in experiments intended to fix the defects of outmoded formalities. To a degree, the gap between formalities and actualities is an inevitable byproduct of adapting to changing circumstances. Informal practices that prove useful may eventually be formalized—as parts of the party system have been in the United States.

Chapter 8

Aspects of Institutional Stewardship

Leaders focus heavily on institutions, because institutions are the means by which life is breathed into governance strategies. Leaders must attend to four tasks: the design and consolidation of new institutions and the administration and adaptation of existing institutions.[1]

Design. By this I mean the intellectual project of deciding how new institutions ought to be structured. Should government be organized as one branch, or two, or three, or four?[2] Should authority be centralized or widely distributed? Should bureaucracies or markets be relied upon for the production of public services? Which state positions should be based on merit, which elected, which filled by patronage, and which filled by other considerations? These are all questions of design and, of course, there are many others.

Leaders and critics outside the state are constantly engaged in debate about institutional design. The pressure to invent new designs is felt most intensely where threats to the state are perceived to be severe—in the field of national defense or internal security, for example. Leaders often borrow designs from powerful or rival states in addition to learning from their own experience. Design thinking is also heavily influenced by technological change. New techniques of surveillance, transportation, and communication; new methods of capturing and using energy; new kinds of weaponry—all of these create new possibilities for the exercise of authority and induce innovations in institutional design. Of course, there is extensive literature that examines the processes by which ideas about design evolve—ranging from histories of political thought to more concrete work on policy diffusion, policy learning, and technological innovation.

Consolidation. This term is often used by experts in peacebuilding and statebuilding—that is, the job of shoring up fragile states. Timothy Sisk suggests that consolidation is best understood as the antonym of fragility.[3] Consolidation has also been described as the process of solidifying or "locking in" new arrangements. There is probably no significant difference between consolidation and the older term used by sociologists, institutionalization, which is defined as the "process by which organizations and procedures acquire value and stability."[4] Institutions are institutions precisely because they appear to be made up of durable patterns of conduct.

We can talk about consolidation at different levels—about the locking-in of an entire state or major aspects of the state ("democratic consolidation," for example) or about specific laws, organizations, programs, and practices. In any case, the prerequisites for consolidation are similar. People must have new institutions explained to them. They must understand what these institutions are supposed to accomplish, how they are supposed to work, and what duties they impose. People must also be persuaded about the value of new institutions. Leaders cultivate respect and even love for basic laws like the U.S. Constitution, and a similar process goes on within specific organizations, as employees are induced to accept the mission and values of a new enterprise.

People must also be persuaded that new institutions will endure. To borrow a term from economics, leaders must make a "credible commitment" to new arrangements.[5] This encourages citizens and businesses to make their own commitments—for example, by acquiring specialized training or sinking capital into private organizations that work closely with public institutions. Often, private actors must make costly investments for public institutions to work well. For example, the rule of law depends on lawyers, law schools, and bar associations as well as on courts and police forces. Similarly, public schools only work when people choose to become trained as teachers and there are colleges to provide them with training. When private actors make such commitments, they have an interest in the survival of public institutions. As a consequence, these new institutions become more durable.[6]

Administration. Once established, institutions must be administered. I could also say that they must be managed. Administration encompasses the running of organizations, the enforcement of laws, and the execution of programs. Luther Gulick was concentrating on problems of administration in 1937 when he attempted to distill "the work of the chief executive" by offering the acronym POSDCORB: planning, organizing, staffing, directing, coordinating, reporting, and budgeting.[7] As noted in the introduction, this aspect of public administration has also dominated the attention of scholars in the Western world over the last two generations. The broad architecture of government, the institutional infrastructure that makes it possible for agencies to get on with their work, has largely been taken for granted. The emphasis has instead been on the effective use of resources within agencies and programs. As James Q. Wilson observed, "Public management . . . is a world of settled institutions."[8] Laurence Lynn made the same point in 2006: "Management is concerned with the organizations that conduct the actual operations of government *within an institutional framework*."[9]

Adaptation. The final aspect of institutional stewardship is adaptation: the renovation or reform of institutions in response to changing conditions.[10] This is not simply a reprise of design and consolidation. Effective adaptation also requires perceptivity, to see that circumstances are changing and that the current governance strategy and institutional complex are no longer fit for the purpose. Similarly, it requires the ability to speculate about the future, to estimate whether a mismatch of strategy and circumstances is likely to get worse. Adaptation also implies the abandonment of old routines. This can be difficult when there is a strong prevailing belief in the value of existing institutions or when individuals have made substantial investments on the assumption that institutions will persist for a long time.

The notion that the state requires unceasing renovation is an old one. Thomas Jefferson observed that institutions must change to "keep pace with the times."[11] A century later, the pragmatist philosopher John Dewey agreed that the formation of states was "an experimental process," that every state is constantly "rediscovered [and] re-made."[12] Dewey's contemporary, R. M. MacIver, said that "the state has no finality, can have no perfected form."[13] MacIver believed that the evolution of institutions often proceeded rapidly.

"Government," he wrote in 1946, "is subject to great transformations within a single generation."[14]

In fact, there is a divide among scholars about the plasticity of state institutions—that is, about the ease with which they can be reformed to suit new conditions. Within the field of international relations, many writers assume that institutions are malleable, that they can be reshaped easily as circumstances change. These writers see a world in flux, in which the unceasing adaptation of strategies and institutions is essential to survival.[15] This process of adaptation has an external and internal aspect. Externally, adaptation requires the adjustment of those institutions that regulate relationships between states. "In a dynamic world in which forces shift and ideas change," Nicolas Spykman said in 1942, "no legal structure can remain acceptable for any length of time."[16] Indeed, many students of international relations describe "radical changes" or "great transformations" in the structure of the international system over time.[17] The internal arrangements of states are also perceived to change substantially in response to shifts in international politics. States are regarded as "dynamic phenomena."[18] The rapid redesign of American institutions after the advent of the Cold War provides one illustration of this dynamism. In scarcely more than a decade, the United States "set new political objectives, developed new military capabilities, devised new diplomatic techniques, invented new instruments of foreign operations . . . [and shifted power from] an increasingly acquiescent Congress into an increasingly imperial Presidency."[19] In other words, the architecture of the American state was thoroughly overhauled.

Not all scholars share this view about the plasticity of institutions. In the last three decades, many students of domestic American politics have taken the contrary position: that institutions are rigid, even dangerously so. Many scholars working in the domain known as the "new institutionalism" recognize that state institutions often require adjustments because of changing circumstances, but they question whether these adjustments are made with sufficient speed. Two early advocates of the new institutionalism, James March and Johan Olsen, challenged the view that institutions "evolve through some form of historical efficient process" in response to "current environmental conditions."[20] The reality, they said, was inefficiency: most of the time, "the rate of change [of an institution] is likely to be inconsistent with the rate of change in the environment to which the institution is adapting."[21]

This has been distilled into the proposition that institutions are "sticky." Stickiness, as Francis Fukuyama has explained, means that institutions "are changed only with great difficulty. . . . Institutions that are created to meet one set of conditions often survive even when those conditions change or disappear."[22] Severe stickiness leads to "political decay," which Fukuyama says is the main problem of contemporary American governance.[23]

Other scholars have taken a similarly dire view about the rigidity of the American state. Mancur Olson warned in 1982 that advanced liberal democracies like the United States are prone to an "institutional sclerosis" that prevents adaptation to changing circumstances.[24] Many factors are said to contribute to stickiness or sclerosis: a shortage of professionals capable of monitoring and predicting social trends, electoral processes that encourage attention to short-run concerns, and a defect in human nature that makes it difficult to take the long view. But the factor that is typically emphasized is the obstructive power of vested interests—that is, groups that benefit from the status quo. This was Olson's view. A follower of Olson, Jonathan Rauch, redefined sclerosis as "creeping special-interest gridlock."[25] Like Olson, Rauch believed that democratic states were especially prone to this disease.

Which is the more accurate view: plasticity or rigidity? This is a question that deserves more attention than it has received. Too often, writers in both camps simply adopt their premise—either plasticity or rigidity—without scrutinizing it too closely. On close examination, we begin to realize that it is hard to define concepts like plasticity or rigidity. How do we decide when change ought to happen and whether change is happening with adequate speed? One thing that can be agreed upon is that judgments about plasticity will be affected by the timeframe used for analysis. If we take a long view, spanning decades or more, as writers in international relations tend to do, then we are more likely to see plasticity. If we take a short view, perhaps a decade or two, we are more likely to see rigidity. Human beings are naturally inclined to take a short view: they judge based on their recent memory.[26]

We should also recognize an unavoidable tension between two aspects of institutional stewardship: consolidation and adaptation. At the stage of consolidation, we try to make routines last indefinitely. To borrow a phrase from Arnold Toynbee, we try to cultivate the "mirage of immortality."[27] We want people to believe wholeheartedly in institutions, so much so that institutions are taken for granted and cooperation with their demands is automatic. As noted earlier, we also want people to become materially invested in the status quo. At the stage of adaptation, however, the table turns. We ask people to question old assumptions and abandon significant material investments. Once regarded as virtues, ideological and financial commitments are now seen as vices that contribute to sclerosis and decay. This tension between consolidation and adaptation can be managed, but it cannot be avoided completely. Some techniques for managing the tension are discussed in chapter 18.

Chapter 9

CHALLENGES IN STRATEGY-MAKING

A strategy for governing is an overall plan that describes how state activities will be organized to achieve a particular set of goals, given the circumstances confronting leaders at a particular moment in history. Crafting a sound strategy is hard work, and strategies vary widely in quality. Some are so poorly reasoned and blind to circumstances that they lead to the replacement of leaders and even the collapse of states.

Leaders encounter five difficulties while crafting strategies for governing. The first is conflict between the goals identified in chapter 5. Ideally, leaders would like to achieve all goals simultaneously. But this is rarely possible. More often than not, attainment of one goal means compromise of another. Consequently, leaders must set priorities; they must decide which goals matter more. And priorities are often contingent: what matters more depends on the conditions prevailing at a particular moment in history.

A familiar conflict of goals is that between internal order and human rights. Obviously, we would like to have domestic peace and justice at the same time. But there are moments when liberties must be restricted to restore order: authorities detain people and suspend habeas corpus, or undertake more intrusive searches and surveillance, or impose tighter restrictions on travel and mass gatherings. When the crisis passes, liberties may be restored. Some constitutions explicitly recognize the possibility that *states of emergency* may arise that require this recalibration of priorities. These constitutions stipulate when and how long civil liberties can be restricted. The constitutions of some other countries do not explicitly anticipate states of emergency. But de facto states of emergency still arise, as one did in the United States after the terrorist attacks of September 11, 2001. In any case, it is difficult to articulate clear rules about how states of emergency should be managed: it is a matter of judgment, contingent on facts about the character and severity of the threat to order.

Another conflict among goals arises between external security and internal order. Leaders often need robust military capabilities, especially in times of actual war, and as a result they may need to make heavy demands on society to support their armed forces. It may be necessary to introduce conscription or, in other words, to force people to work for the state. (The United States maintained a system of conscription for one-third of the twentieth century.) Governments also expropriate property: they impose taxes to finance military activity, force citizens to lend to the state on unfavorable terms, and take control of factories. Governments may also destroy private wealth through inflation, if they finance military activities by printing more money. All of this activity may weaken popular support for the state. Conscription can lead to draft riots and mutinies, while policies that destroy private wealth can lead to protests, rebellions, and black markets. Governments constantly wrestle with this tension between external security and internal order. They use propaganda to build support for military activity, promise benefits to the public when war ends, reduce the need for conscription by shifting to labor-saving military technologies, and distribute military spending in ways that build support for the armed services. Or governments may simply limit military commitments overseas to keep peace at home, as the United States did in the 1970s following protests over the Vietnam War.

The desire to promote economic growth may collide with several other goals, such as national security, internal order, and human rights. In the 1990s, conventional wisdom said that the best way to spur economic growth was by deregulation, free trade, international investment, and increased immigration. This formula appeared to foster growth. After 2001, however, dangers of this approach became evident in the United States. A policy of open borders made it easier for terrorists to enter the country, while deregulation made it harder to safeguard infrastructure against terrorist attacks. As international tensions revived in the 2000s, U.S. leaders also became uneasy about their dependence on countries like China. At the same time, a laissez-faire economic policy contributed to rising inequality and more financial crashes, which, in turn, led to protests and political turmoil. Critics complained that the American political system had been turned into a plutocracy—a system of rule by the rich, for the rich—thereby undermining the right of the people to participate equally in the government.[1] By 2016, the tradeoffs contained within the prevailing governance strategy had become intolerable: leaders were searching for a new way to reconcile economic growth with the goals of external security, internal order, and human rights.

A second challenge in crafting governance strategies is uncertainty about the techniques to use to achieve goals. Even when leaders are clear about their priorities, they may be unsure about the most effective ways to pursue them. The military strategist Carl von Clausewitz wrote in the nineteenth century that decision-making during wartime is usually "hidden more or less in the clouds of great uncertainty."[2] This observation should not be limited to wartime. All aspects of governance are enveloped in clouds of uncertainty. Every day, leaders struggle to influence social systems whose dimensions and dynamics are poorly understood. As we shall see in the next chapter, a large part of state action is aimed at dispelling such uncertainty. Leaders try to map the territory, both literally and metaphorically, to gain a better sense of what tactics will likely succeed. But this project can never be finished, because the territory is vast and constantly changing. As a result, leaders are forced to act on incomplete information and imperfect theories about the way the world works. "The tragic aspect of policymaking," Henry Kissinger has observed, "lies precisely in its unavoidable component of conjecture."[3]

Leaders constantly roll the dice as they decide how to pursue goals. In 1989, Chinese leaders were confronted with a massive student protest in Tiananmen Square in central Beijing. The students wanted more freedoms. China's rulers agreed on their own priorities, which were to maintain internal stability and continue Communist Party rule. But they split on tactics. One side thought that the way to restore order was by making concessions to the students. The other side pointed out that rulers in the Soviet bloc were making concessions without obtaining peace and that granting a few liberties only produced demands for more. This latter group favored a crackdown on dissent. The counterargument was that a crackdown might only inflame the population. The uncertainties were ineluctable: either path was essentially a gamble. The hard-line faction won out in 1989, and their gamble has appeared to pay off. Since 1989, Chinese leaders have maintained internal order by repressing dissent, appeasing citizens with rapid economic growth, and distracting them with nationalist rhetoric. But this path is still a gamble, and some observers wonder whether Chinese leaders have only delayed the day of reckoning. They think that long-term stability will require political liberalization.[4]

This Chinese dilemma about tactics is universal. Machiavelli himself addressed it when he wondered whether it was better for a prince to be feared or loved.[5] Even in liberal democracies, leaders make choices between conciliation and coercion, although they typically avoid the extreme options available to leaders in authoritarian states. In the 1910s, for example, American lawmakers debated whether militant suffragism and labor radicalism would be staunched more quickly by policy concessions or criminal prosecutions. In the 1960s, American politics was seized again with the question of whether internal peace would be achieved more readily by giving way to protesters or emphasizing law and order. And at the end of the twentieth century, American leaders debated whether the anti-globalization movement was better managed by slowing down trade liberalization or employing tougher policing of protests. Of course, it is possible in each of these cases to make a moral argument about the path that ought to be pursued. But leaders are also making a tactical judgment about which path is more likely to restore peace and order, and this judgment is always wrapped in Clausewitz's cloud of uncertainty.

Even more uncertainty envelops decisions about the economy. All leaders want to achieve rapid growth, for the reasons identified in chapter 5. But there is never clarity about the best way of doing this. In the 1980s, a Canadian politician captured the predicament when he said that the decision to sign a free trade treaty with the United States depended ultimately on a "leap of faith."[6] This is true of all major decisions about the economy. Leaders try to shape vast and protean systems of production, trade, and finance, which involve the interactions of millions of people. The effect of government policies is difficult to predict, and unintended consequences are commonplace. This uncertainty about cause and effect is one reason why states have pursued radically different methods of cultivating their economies. There is no clear path to prosperity. Some states have developed elaborate plans for economic development, taken control of key industries, imposed strict limits on overseas trade and finance, and forced their way into foreign markets. Other states are skeptical about the feasibility or wisdom of detailed plans, state control, autarkism, and force.

Uncertainty explains variation in economic policies over time as well as the tendency of economic experts to oscillate between hubris and self-doubt. In 1955, for example, one analyst boasted that the American economy had "left every other system in recorded history immeasurably far behind. Its rate of progress shows no sign of slackening."[7] By the 1970s, however, experts were flummoxed by the arrival of economic stagnation. Policies that were celebrated in the 1950s, it was now declared, simply did not work.[8] The Reagan era marked a significant shift in economic policy, and hubris returned by the end of the 1990s. Experts were convinced that they had rediscovered the formula of sustained prosperity. But this confidence was shattered again after the financial crisis of 2008.

A third challenge in crafting governance strategies is managing cultural and institutional inheritances.[9] Leaders never work on a clean slate. As Karl Marx said in 1851, "Men make their own history, but they do not make it just as they please in circumstances they choose for themselves; rather they make it in present circumstances, given and inherited."[10] Typically, leaders govern populations that have settled understandings about the way that life should be organized. In such societies, there are well-established routines for managing everyday interactions. It is impossible to change all of these understandings and routines at once. This is true whether specific institutions are "sticky"—that is, hard to change—or malleable. Even without stickiness, leaders can accomplish only so much work within their lifetimes. This fact constrains the discretion of leaders in crafting a strategy for governing.

Leaders must wrestle with constraints imposed by history and decide how ambitious they should be. Some have attempted root-and-branch reforms, but such revolutionary projects often fail catastrophically, resulting in the death of millions.[11] Conservatives are more skeptical about the feasibility and wisdom of wide-ranging reforms. An implication of the conservative viewpoint is that the governance strategy pursued by one generation of leaders will be dictated largely by the strategic choices made by earlier generations. Strategy-making, in this view, consists largely of adjustment on the edges. But even then, leaders must make difficult calculations. They must decide which aspects of the prevailing strategy are most in need of reform and which can be left alone. And they must decide how to achieve that reform—whether by subtle amendment or a frontal assault on the status quo. They may pursue a policy of experimentation, as Franklin Roosevelt did in the 1930s, to learn more about how reform can be achieved and how far it can really go.

The fourth challenge in crafting governance strategies derives from turbulence in the governing environment. Some aspects of the environment may remain relatively constant, but other aspects change quickly. This can throw a leader's calculations into disarray. Much time is spent in deciding which goals are most important and which methods most likely to be effective, given the circumstances. But even while these decisions are being made, circumstances are changing. Maybe a surprise attack requires a recalibration of thinking about the relative importance of security and liberty, or a technological innovation undermines the capacity of government agencies to monitor and regulate private action. Market forces—what Joseph Schumpeter called the "perennial gale of creative destruction"[12]—may cause the collapse or relocation of an entire industry. An unexpected alteration in fertility rates or patterns of disease may affect the size and health of the population. And patterns of settlement and social organization are constantly mutating as well.[13]

Leaders try to cope with this turbulence as they design strategies and institutions. One temptation is to impose rigid controls on social and economic affairs so that turbulence is eliminated and change only happens on a schedule set by the state. This approach crushes freedom and ultimately fails, if only because some factors simply cannot be controlled, such as the behavior of people and governments outside the state's territory. Another technique for managing turbulence is to improve the state's capacity to anticipate events—that is, to know the future. I will discuss this in the next chapter. Leaders may also try to manage turbulence by equivocating about priorities, putting off major decisions, and hedging their bets with duplicative or contradictory policies. But this sort of behavior may be perceived as indecisive leadership, a perception that can undermine attempts by leaders to consolidate their policies. On the other hand, an effort to look decisive—by making excessively strong commitments to policies and denying the reality of turbulence—has its own dangers: leaders may hobble their capacity to adapt as circumstances change.

The final challenge in crafting governance strategies is analytic complexity—that is, the difficulty of absorbing knowledge and making judgments about large and complicated questions. In the twentieth century, one of the main aspirations of administrative reform was to build institutions that could support leaders in crafting their overall plans. An early model for top-level administrative reform was the general staffs set up to support military planning in many Western states at the end of the nineteenth century. By the 1960s, most executives in Western states had similar staffs to guide economic and social planning, coordinate the flow of advice to leaders, assure that choices were thoroughly considered, and monitor the implementation of decisions. Many governments struggled to develop decision-making processes that were comprehensive without being cumbersome.[14] In the early twenty-first century, governments are trying to adapt these processes to a world in which information flows are even deeper and harder to manage and in which the pace of events has accelerated.[15]

Obviously, the personal qualities of leaders are important as well. The process of strategy-making is not easy when the leader proves to be a "f**king moron."[16] Experience is also helpful. Defenders of the current Chinese regime argue that Western democracies have a bad habit of electing amateurs to top positions, while the Chinese system, although non-democratic, selects leaders with a solid record of accomplishment.[17] Training also matters. I noted earlier that leaders engage in a distinctive mode of reasoning, *raison d'état*, which relates to the skillful crafting of governance strategies. This mode of reasoning can be recognized and cultivated. One criticism of public affairs schools in the United States is that they have neglected this very subject. These schools often claim to prepare students for leadership, but they do not provide the theoretical equipment necessary to handle the biggest and toughest problems that leaders encounter. I will discuss this in more detail in chapter 21.

Chapter 10

The Struggle for Mastery

An observer of contemporary Russian politics has observed, "Authoritarian regimes yearn for control—to stem the flow of ideas and to manage events. But this is infinitely more difficult these days. Instead, they find themselves hostage to circumstances, often forced to respond in ways they never anticipated, and struggling in vain to hold on to illusions of stability, greatness, and power."[1] In fact, we can say this about all regimes, democratic as well as authoritarian. Leaders in every state "yearn for control" and design institutions to fulfill that yearning. The critical difference is that liberal democratic regimes are designed to regulate that impulse: the institutional complex includes constraints on what leaders can do in their drive to achieve control over circumstances.

In fact, yearning for control is not always a bad thing. Leaders in democratic societies often seek control because they want to serve their people. Without adequate control over circumstances, leaders cannot guarantee the safety of citizens, fairness in the marketplace, or equal access to essential services. The complaint of progressive reformers in the United States in the early part of the twentieth century was that American leaders lacked sufficient control over their environment and that people were suffering as a result. It is difficult today to appreciate the feebleness of government in major Western states only a century ago. In 1914, a prominent writer complained that American politicians suffered from "a conscious impotence." The country was in turmoil, but its leaders seemed "to have as little to do with all these changes, as little ability to foresee or avert or resist them, as the farmer, who sees approaching the tornado which will uproot his crop, has power to stay its devastating course."[2] It seemed that leaders were simply swept along by events. Walter Lippmann said in 1914 that the United States faced a choice between "drift and mastery" in a world of "brain-splitting complexity."[3] Lippmann wanted leaders to gain control, to establish mastery over their circumstances, so that the potential of American democracy could be realized. The field of public administration was invented to achieve this goal.

Before he was president of the United States, or commander-in-chief of the Continental army, or an officer in the colonial British army, George Washington was a land surveyor. As a sixteen-year-old, he was sent into the Virginia wilderness to map the territory. This experience shaped his entire career. As a general, Washington had a particular talent for gauging the terrain on which battles would be fought. As president, he stocked his office with maps and charts, and when he traveled, "he methodically recorded the topographical features of places, as if he remained a working surveyor."[4] Washington once said that skill in surveying was essential for the owner of any large estate, "the bounds of some part or other of which is always in controversy."[5] He might have said the same about military and civilian leadership. Especially at that time, governing was made complicated by ignorance about the terrain begin governed.

For leaders, the first aspect of mastery consists of knowing the territory over which sovereignty is claimed. Today, in the age of satellite imaging, we take this sort of knowledge for granted. Two centuries ago, leaders did not. They could not identify precisely the boundaries of their lands, the paths of major rivers, or the routes by which traders or troops could traverse the country. Such ignorance triggered border conflicts, slowed settlement, and complicated the task of maintaining order. Leaders tried to dispel this ignorance by creating the capacity within government to map the land, coasts, and waterways. This was harder than you might think. The Mississippi River had to be remapped frequently because it constantly shifts its course. This is a good metaphor for the larger challenge of understanding the domain over which sovereignty is asserted.

The impulse to know the territory was carried into other areas in which the ignorance of leaders was equally profound. Governments mapped the climate by describing patterns of temperature, precipitation, sunshine, and storm activity. They conducted censuses to know how many people lived in their country, where they lived, and what kind of people they were. Next, they mapped economic activity—patterns of production, trade, and finance. Then they mapped information flows—the volume and sometimes even the content of communications. The rapid expansion of digital surveillance activities by U.S. government agencies after the terrorist attacks of September 11, 2001 was simply another manifestation of the centuries-long drive to dispel ignorance about the territory being governed. For a few months in 2003, the administration of President George W. Bush operated an antiterrorism program called Total Information Awareness. The label was alarming but also apt. The struggle for mastery begins with the search for information.[6]

The next step toward mastery is gaining a deeper understanding of the environment in which states operate. In the nineteenth century, people began to perceive the world as a composite of systems governed by laws that could be revealed through scientific inquiry.[7] By the late nineteenth century, for example, it was not satisfactory just to describe weather patterns. The ambition was to explain how weather systems work, so that it was possible to forecast what the weather would be. Similarly, the notion of an economic system emerged, the precursor of the modern concept of the economy, and experts attempted to explain its cycles of boom and bust. Similarly, researchers examined the dynamics of fertility, mortality, and migration within human populations, while history was parsed to explain the dynamics of conflict within the state system. Governments have always been important sponsors as well as active consumers of such research. Leaders appreciate that the world cannot be governed until its mechanisms are exposed.

Mastery requires more than information and understanding, however. Leaders need tools to influence the dynamics of systems; or, in other words, to influence circumstances. People outside the state apparatus need to be induced to change their behavior, whether by persuasion, material inducement, or threat of punishment. Whatever the preferred method of influence, leaders must have the administrative capacity to apply it: they must establish their own bureaucracies or delegate responsibilities to other public or private organizations.

Two hundred years ago, the administrative capabilities of American government were primitive. The federal government had fewer than five thousand employees: today, the Wal-Mart corporation employs more people than that in the state of Maine alone. By 2017, the federal government had about two million civilian employees and about 1.4 million active-duty military personnel. Federal money also supports the employment of millions of people by state and local government and private sector contractors. This expansion of administrative capabilities has vastly improved the ability of government to enforce its laws. But it has also generated new problems of monitoring and coordinating behavior within the state apparatus itself. Sometimes, bureaucrats neglect the goals of their superiors and use their authority to advance their own ambitions or make deals with the groups they are supposed to be regulating, and sometimes agencies compete against one another when they ought to be cooperating.

Now and then, leaders adopt policies that exceed their capacity to exercise control. In 1807, President Thomas Jefferson prodded Congress to adopt the Embargo Act, which tried to avoid entanglement in European wars by prohibiting Americans from trading with the rest of the world. This was an ambitious goal for a country whose small population, huddled on the Atlantic seaboard, was dependent on overseas trade and finance. And the policy was a failure. Trade restrictions provoked outrage, especially in New England, where there was talk about secession from the United States. Moreover, federal law could not be enforced. The government could not stop smuggling, despite Jefferson's deployment of the navy and army. President Jefferson conceded that the embargo law was "the most embarrassing one we have ever had to execute. I did not expect a crop of so sudden & rank growth of fraud and open opposition by force could have grown up in the U.S."[8]

An equally audacious attempt at societal control was tried a century later. In 1919 the U.S. Constitution was amended to prohibit the manufacture, importation, and sale of alcoholic beverages within the United States. Advocates of prohibition said that it would save the country from moral ruin. It also meant the destruction of the fifth largest industry in the country. The enforcement machinery of the federal government was expanded but still proved incapable of preventing rampant violations of the law. "In almost every respect imaginable," Daniel Okrent writes, "Prohibition was a failure. It encouraged criminality and institutionalized hypocrisy. It deprived the government of revenue, stripped the gears of the political system, and imposed profound limitations on individual rights."[9] The ban on alcoholic beverages was reversed in 1933.

The trade embargo of 1807 and prohibition in 1919 are examples of governmental overstretch. There are many others, such as the "unconditional war on poverty" declared by President Lyndon Johnson in 1964, the "all-out offensive" against drugs launched by President Richard Nixon in 1971, and the global war to "rid the world of evil-doers" announced by President George W. Bush in 2001. In all of these cases, leaders suffered from overconfidence. They overestimated the extent of their control and their capacity to influence society.[10] One of the main roles of experts in public administration should be to warn leaders against such mistakes, by giving them frank advice about what the administrative apparatus is capable of doing.

Leaders and societies often learn from such mistakes, and even failed policies tend to result in improved administrative capacities. The extent of control enjoyed by leaders today is vastly greater than it was a century ago. At the dawn of the twentieth century, leaders in the richest countries were still largely unaware of what was happening within the borders of their countries. They did not really know what people were doing or why they were doing it, and they had hardly any ability to compel people to alter their conduct. Circumstances are now vastly different. For example, advances in information technology are producing ever-larger amounts of data about the behavior of governed populations. Indeed, the obstacle to mastery may no longer be a dearth of information, as it was in 1900. Today, the obstacle might be a tsunami of information that overwhelms the capacity of leaders to make sense of it and respond appropriately.

Chapter 11

DANGER, STRATEGIC FRAGILITY, AND REALISM

Some scholars who study international relations subscribe to a way of thinking about the world called realism. Realists see the world of states as an anarchical and dangerous place. There is no supreme authority that can enforce international law, protect states from attack, and assure that they are treated fairly. States are understood to live in a "situation of Hobbesian fear."[1] They have no reliable friends. Consequently, leaders must be on guard. They watch for threats from other states, prepare for attacks, and jostle for advantage within the state system. To protect the national interest, realists argue, leaders sometimes have to make choices that would be indefensible by the standards of conventional morality.[2]

Niccolò Machiavelli is considered one of the intellectual godfathers of realism. He saw a world full of hazards. His home, the city-state of Florence, was constantly threatened by neighboring city-states and kingdoms. As a result, Florentine leaders were obsessed with intelligence-gathering and diplomacy, alliances, war preparation, and actual combat. Machiavelli did not take for granted the survival of Florence as an independent city-state.

Machiavelli's critics complained that he was prepared to condone all sorts of misbehavior—deception, lying, betrayal, cruelty—to preserve the state. The ends, he was understood to say, justified the means.

In fact, Machiavelli was not so cold-blooded. He was a humanist and republican who believed that a well-designed state gave people the freedom to pursue a good life.[3] To defend this kind of state, Machiavelli argued, leaders sometimes had to get their hands dirty. Machiavelli did not take this sort of conduct lightly. He believed that leaders were sometimes driven to it by the pressure of circumstances—that is, by the immediacy and severity of the threats confronting the state.

Modern-day realists emphasize threats posed by other states, but Machiavelli had broader concerns. He said a leader should have *two* fears: "one internal, based on his subjects; the other external, based on foreign powers."[4] Other writers of that era emphasized internal dangers as well. Great states, the French jurist Jean Bodin cautioned, "often fall suddenly from their own weight . . . [or] are brought to their ends by internal causes."[5] The English statesman Francis Bacon also warned about domestic "discords, quarrels, and factions." He listed the causes of unrest, many of which are still pertinent today: "innovation in religion; taxes; alteration of laws and customs; breaking of privileges; general oppression; advancement of unworthy persons; strangers; dearths; disbanded soldiers; [and] factions grown desperate."[6] In the eighteenth century, the American founding fathers were equally concerned with "domestic faction and sedition."[7] One of the largest armies ever led directly by George Washington was assembled in 1794 to thwart a rebellion by American citizens, not to fight the British. And the gravest threat to the survival of the United States after 1789 came in the form of civil war, not conflict with another state.

Realists believe that the world is a dangerous place, full of risks to essential state interests, and that leaders must be alert to these risks. The origin of the risk, foreign or domestic, should not be essential to the definition of realism. Experts who study fragile states today, who dwell on the difficulty of restoring peace and order within conflict-ridden societies, are still thinking like realists, even though the danger of attack by other states is negligible.[8] Similarly, writers who worry about the survival of liberal democratic institutions in the United States and other Western countries are realists, because they recognize the fragility of the existing order. In the aftermath of the 2016 presidential election, Paul Krugman asked, "Is America a failed state and society? It looks truly possible."[9] Later Krugman wrote, "The erosion of democratic foundations has been underway for decades, and there's no guarantee that we will ever be able to recover. But if there is any hope of redemption, it will have to begin with a clear recognition of how bad things are. American democracy is very much on the edge."[10] That is the mentality of a realist operating within the realm of domestic affairs.

In fact, threats managed by leaders come in many forms. Writers who emphasize the dangers posed by "unpredictable market forces" are also thinking like realists.[11] So are writers who dwell on technological changes that have created a "new anarchical information environment."[12] And so are experts who worry about how climate change may lead to social conflict and political instability.[13]

Leaders try to manage such dangers by crafting strategies for governing and renovating institutions to give effect to those strategies. They are engaged in the work of threat management. Leaders hope that these strategies will provide long-lasting protection against the most serious dangers, but this hope is often dashed. Events move too quickly and strategies become outmoded. To put it another way, governance strategies are typically fragile. They require constant maintenance and renovation to accommodate an ever-changing array of risks. Leaders may be reluctant to admit this publicly, because it undermines their effort to have their plans taken seriously. The demands of institutional consolidation require that leaders overstate the durability of their strategies. But realism requires an acknowledgment that risks are highly variable and that no single strategy can be effective in managing them for very long.

Over the last century, many scholars in public administration have talked like realists, even if they have not adopted the label. Charles Merriam, one of the main proponents of the new field in the 1930s, warned that without "creative evolution" of public institutions, the United States faced the prospect of a political and social disruption that would be "terrifying to those who love the status quo."[14] Merriam wrote this shortly before he began advising President Franklin Roosevelt on the restructuring of American government. A similar mentality shaped the thinking of the young scholars who called for a "new public administration" in the late 1960s and early 1970s. As one observer noted in 1973, this body of work was produced in an "atmosphere of crisis" and imbued with a "sense of urgency, a feeling of need to change direction."[15] A similar feeling of urgency affects the writing of leading scholars in public administration today. Donald Kettl, for example, has recently warned that American government "is failing to adapt to the challenges it faces" and that this might lead to "the decline and fall of the American republic."[16]

All of these scholars have been committed to the creation of a state that takes liberal-democratic values seriously. Nonetheless, they were all realists. They recognized that the creation and maintenance of such a state is very difficult, because an unruly world constantly upsets carefully wrought plans. Threats to national interests arise from all directions, and good leadership requires vigilance, as well as nimbleness in adapting plans and institutions. The costs of inattention can be substantial because "nothing that gets out of sync with its environment lasts long."[17]

Chapter 12

Time and Progress

As we develop a new approach to research in public administration, we must make a conscious decision about the timeframe that we intend to apply—that is, how far back and forward we are prepared to look. Specifically, we must adopt a longer timeframe than is commonly used by researchers today.

The choice of timeframe—long or short—affects our thinking about governing in many ways. For example, it influences assumptions about the malleability of institutions. If we take a long view, we are more likely to be struck by substantial changes in the design of institutions. Think about the modest role of the U.S. presidency, the small scale of armed forces, or the limited amount of regulation in 1918 compared to 2018. The long view encourages us to think that institutions are malleable. If we look back only five or ten years, however, we will not see nearly as much change. Consequently, we might be more likely to conclude that institutions are inflexible.

The choice of timeframe has other consequences. If we take the long view, we are more likely to recognize those social and economic forces that only operate slowly. Human migration is a good example: large movements of people tend to happen over decades. The rise and fall of great powers also happens over decades rather than a few years. The long view also improves our ability to see patterns in events, avoid surprise, and learn from experience. The financial crisis of 2007–2008 was a shock to those who took the short view, because a crisis of that scale had not happened in the United States and other advanced economies in recent years. It was less of a shock to those who knew about the longer track record of capitalism and its cycles of boom and bust.[1] Similarly, by taking the long view, we recognize that devastating pandemics are a familiar part of the human experience. We could say the same about massive weather disasters, although climate change is now shifting this category of events from the exceptional to the routine even within the short view of history.

We must adopt a similarly long timeframe when looking into the future. What will happen next, and what should we prepare for? The answers to these questions differ markedly if we are looking five years into the future or thirty years. A long view into the future heightens our sensitivity to danger, because there is a higher probability of a calamity (another crash, another pandemic) occurring in that longer period of time. But a longer view might also make us more optimistic about our capacity to adjust strategy and institutions in anticipation of those dangers.

Scholars often make tacit assumptions about the appropriate timeframe for research, and these assumptions sometimes vary markedly between disciplines. Scholars in international relations tend to take the long view. No understanding of that domain is possible, Hendrick Spruyt has recently argued, without a study of the past.[2] Historians also take the long view, although critics of that discipline believe there has been a shortening of vision in recent years. Jo Guldi and David Armitage have complained that American historians are succumbing to short-termism or presentism: "Historians once told arching stories of scale but, nearly forty years ago, many if not most of them stopped doing so. For two generations, between about 1975 and 2005, they conducted most of their studies on biological time-spans of between five and fifty years, approximating the length of a mature human life."[3] The discipline of political science has also been criticized for presentism. While some scholars working in the subfield of American political development (APD) have argued that processes of state formation can only be understood by looking at the long course of history, they are a minority within the discipline.[4] Most research within political science appears to focus on developments within the past ten or twenty years—again, within the life experience of a working scholar.[5]

Presentism is a serious problem in the discipline of public administration as well. This was not always so. In the 1940s, administrative history—the study of processes "by which agencies come into existence, undergo changes as to organizational form or functions, and are absorbed or liquidated"— was an essential part of the research program in public administration.[6] Lynton Caldwell insisted in 1955 that the study of administration was necessarily historical, because history provided the only means "of discovering how factors in the environment condition organizational behavior and what types of organizational adaptation have proved successful."[7] But interest in administrative history declined sharply after the 1960s. By the 1990s, research in public administration was routinely criticized for lack of historical consciousness.[8] The past, Christopher Pollitt observed in 2008, "has been squeezed out of contemporary academic treatments of public management."[9] Jos Raadschelders agreed in 2010: "The study of public administration pays little attention to history. . . . Systematic training in research and methods of administrative history is sorely missing."[10]

Why does so much scholarship tend toward presentism? Maybe researchers feel institutional pressure to explore new terrain, with the result that they are drawn to unfolding events rather than to "old news." Presentism could also be a result of methodological biases; for example, when researchers prefer to work with large amounts of quantitative data that are not available for large-scale processes or decades-old events. Or presentism might be a defect of human nature, one of several cognitive biases that compromise the everyday reasoning of academics and non-academics alike. In the late 1970s, the financial analyst Peter Miller suggested that ordinary investors often suffer from "retrospective myopia"; that is, they assume that the future can be predicted based on the experience of the preceding few years alone.[11] This habit of fixating on the "remembered past" affects judgments about politics as well.[12] Arthur Schlesinger suggested that for most people, history begins only at the moment when their political consciousness is awakened, at the beginning of their adult life.[13] That means that the average American has a historical perspective that spans about twenty years. Indeed, some political scientists suggest that retrospective myopia among voters is even shorter than that.[14]

Whatever the cause, we should be aware of the tendency toward presentism and guard against it. States, institutions, and social forces are not people. They do not necessarily rise or fall within the span of a human life or within the even shorter timeframe of a single human memory.[15] If we do not work hard to resist presentism, we will overlook long-term processes that are important in shaping the behavior of today's leaders. We will also underestimate the plasticity of states as well as the transitory character of governance strategies and the institutional complexes that give expression to them.

There is another assumption that shapes our thinking about the evolution of states: the idea of progress—or, in other words, the expectation that governance strategies will generate continual improvement in human welfare.[16] This idea has prevailed in the West since the eighteenth century. It is associated with the rise of science, advances in technology, and improvements in large-scale organization. We have learned more about the world around us and become more confident about our capacity to apply that knowledge in ways that will allow people to live a good life. Advances in human well-being over the last three hundred years—in health, education, and opportunities for creative expression—have been extraordinary. We have come to regard such advances as the natural state of affairs.

However, people have not always subscribed to the idea of progress, especially in the domain of politics. Ancient Greek philosophers did not believe in it. Plato thought that governments proceeded through a neverending cycle: democracies degenerated into mob rule and were replaced by aristocracies, which degenerated into oligarchies, which were replaced by monarchies, which degenerated into tyrannies, which were replaced by democracies, and so on, ad infinitum. Machiavelli, writing in the sixteenth century, appeared to accept Plato's view about the cyclical character of politics.[17] In the eighteenth century, writers now counted as pioneers of the Enlightenment still subscribed to a relatively pessimistic view about human advancement. Great civilizations, it was held, could not sustain themselves forever: eventually they would become corrupt and collapse, so that people would revert to a more primitive way of life. In this view, a successful leader was one who simply slowed the rate of decay.

This element of fatalism was purged from everyday thinking by the early twentieth century. It was replaced by faith in progress through the application of reason. Charles Beard wrote in 1932 that the ancient Greek theory of cycles had been "destroyed by patent facts." Humanity was learning how to use technology to achieve a "conquest of the earth, with a view to raising the standard of life, decreasing the death rate, overcoming illiteracy, eliminating physical suffering, and providing the comforts of a rational living." Beard said that statesmen and citizens alike were now seized with the "doctrine of development."[18] Many American social scientists in the decades following World War II subscribed enthusiastically to this doctrine. They defined their task as understanding and accelerating the process of political and economic modernization.[19] The long economic boom enjoyed by many countries in the postwar years encouraged the belief that humanity had placed itself decisively on the path to continual improvement.

Western faith in the idea of progress has been badly shaken twice in the last fifty years. One moment of self-doubt came in the 1970s, as the postwar economic boom came to an end and social disorder in the advanced democracies increased. A feeling of malaise swept over the United States and other advanced democracies. A contributor for the *New York Times* wrote in 1974 that "The political 'decline of the West' is no longer a subject for theoretical debate, but an ominous reality."[20] This malaise dissipated in the 1980s and 1990s, as economies recovered and the Cold War ended. By the end of the twentieth century, writers were celebrating the triumph of liberal democracy once again. But malaise crept back in during the twenty-first century, especially after the global financial crisis of 2007–2008. By 2016, anxiety about the decline of the West was back in full force. One writer worried that "the most fundamental pillars of the West" were wobbling: "Citizens believe less and less that their systems are able to deliver positive outcomes."[21]

The experience of the last century shows that the idea of progress is subject to its own cycles of boom and bust. These cycles are aggravated by our propensity to retrospective myopia. If the last few years have gone well, we boast about the ascendency of Western civilization. If the last few years have gone badly, we anguish about its decline. A longer view of history encourages a more temperate view of progress. Conditions of life in Western countries are radically better than they were a half century or a century ago. But progress is not incessant: there are fits and starts, advances and setbacks. Herbert Butterfield took this position in 1931, just as Charles Beard was celebrating the inexorable conquest of nature. History, he said, shows "how crooked and perverse the ways of progress are, with what willfulness and waste it twists and turns, and takes anything but the straight track to its goal, and how often it seems to go astray, and to be deflected by any conjuncture, to return to us—if it does return—by a back door."[22]

It is possible to connect this more temperate view of progress with our conversation about governance strategies. All strategies are imperfect. Leaders try to devise ways of advancing national goals given the circumstances. But their decisions are plagued by uncertainty, and circumstances always change. Eventually, even the best plans exhaust their usefulness. Policies that once seemed to produce good results—improved security, prosperity, and social welfare—no longer have that effect. This is what happened in the 1970s and is happening again today. In other words, these moments of malaise can also be interpreted at moments of strategic exhaustion. In these periods, progress appears to have stalled. Leaders and citizens are then plunged into a debate about how national strategy should be recrafted to fit new realities. These periods of strategic readjustment may last for one or two decades, but eventually a new strategy—a new conventional wisdom about governance—appears to emerge. And at this point, the engine of progress starts up again.[23]

Chapter 13

Unexceptionalism

Presentism is not the only habit of thought that compromises our ability to think clearly about strategies for governing in the United States. Another is the doctrine of exceptionalism: the idea that there is something unique about governance in the American context. This mistaken belief makes it harder to learn from the experience of other states.

Faith in American exceptionalism is deeply rooted in some corners of American political science—particularly so in American political development (APD), the subfield of political science most directly concerned with the long-term development of the American state. Ira Katznelson argues that the idea of exceptionalism has been "at the substantive core" of APD since its start almost forty years ago.[1] Another scholar has observed that "work in the APD genre has remained, to some considerable extent, an inquiry to American exceptionalism."[2] The United States has been identified as the "great anomaly among Western states" for several reasons: a political culture hostile to big government, political institutions that fragment authority, sharp regional variations in economic and social conditions, and other "distinctly

American phenomena" such as "social flux, easy access to land, and the sheer size of the 'republic' to be governed."[3]

We should be skeptical about the claim of American exceptionality. The United States is usually contrasted with major Western European states—especially the United Kingdom, Germany, France, and Italy—where it is assumed that circumstances have allowed the emergence of more durable and powerful public institutions. But American observers, looking from a distance, often have overestimated the stability and internal cohesion of these states. Of these four Western European states, three are actually younger than the United States, and all have undergone revolution or radical constitutional reform.[4] Social flux, regional antipathies, and popular resistance to authority are chronic problems for European leaders, just as they are for American leaders.

It is also unreasonable to compare the United States to Western Europe alone, in the way that proponents of exceptionalism usually do. Maybe such a comparison made sense in the nineteenth century, when Western Europe formed the core of the state system. But the world has moved on. Today there are more than one hundred ninety states, of which only two dozen are in Western Europe. The modern state system includes frontier states such as Russia, Brazil, and Canada, in which central governments have struggled to extend their rule over newly acquired territory.[5] It includes superstates such as China, India, and Indonesia, whose vast populations are cleaved by religion, language, history, and class. It includes dozens of fragile states in which "subnational entities are sufficiently powerful to resist and operate autonomously" from national government.[6] And it includes new states created since World War II in which statebuilding has been constrained by the commitment to human rights and free markets.[7] The United States has challenges in common with all of these groups. At different times, it has been a frontier state, a superstate, a fragile state, and a "liberal absolutist" state.[8] In none of these respects has it been exceptional.

There is a temptation to suggest that the United States is exceptional only because of the emphasis that Americans put on their own exceptionality. But even this is not true. People in most countries see something special about their own circumstances. In the nineteenth century, Britons were equally certain about the distinctiveness of their political culture and institutions: about their "exceptional moral character," talent for good government, and commitment to liberal principles.[9] Today, Russian thinkers emphasize the notion of *spetsifika*, or "specialness": the unusual combination of cultural and geographic conditions that shape governance in that country. "All peoples are unique," one journalist observed in 2000, "but Russians think they are more unique than the others."[10] Similarly, Chinese intellectuals dwell on China's status as a "unique civilizational state, [with] its own logic and cycles of development."[11] And Indian writers are convinced of the "unique complexity" of politics in their own country.[12] There is a deeply rooted feeling of "Indian exceptionalism," says Aparna Pande, a sense that India is "special and an example for the rest of the world."[13]

The feeling of exceptionality is shared almost universally, and rightly so. Conditions facing leaders in any one state are different from those facing any other state. Governance strategies must fit those conditions, and consequently we should expect policies and institutions to vary as well. This is why we should be wary about "one size fits all" prescriptions for governmental reform.[14] Moreover, this sort of exceptionalism is a temporal as well as a geographic reality. Conditions in every state change over time. Even supposedly durable elements may vary: histories are rewritten, cultures are transformed, and even climate and geography are altered. Every generation of leaders can make a claim of exceptionality against other generations, even though all have governed the same territory.

Still, we should not get too carried away with this emphasis on variation. Even if circumstances change, there is one important commonality: leaders in all states, at all points in time, deal with the realities of building and maintaining a state. A common set of goals occupies the attention of leaders, even though leaders may not rank those goals in similar ways. All leaders of states engage in a distinctive form of reasoning, *raison d'état*, which is concerned with deciding which goals are most important, and finding clever ways to pursue those goals given the circumstances. We can compare how leaders engage in this reasoning—in other words, how they craft, execute, and revise strategies of governance—even if each leader does this under distinctive conditions.

PART II

Dilemmas in Strategy-Making

Chapter 14

Efficiency or Extravagance

Leaders do their best to make governing look effortless, but it is actually hard work. As they design and implement strategies for governing, leaders must reconcile conflicting goals, wrestle with massive uncertainties and stubborn constraints, and adjust to shifting terrain. Recurrent problems arise when leaders do this work—dilemmas in the making of governance strategies that come up over and over again. In the following chapters, I will look at five of these dilemmas, though there are many more.

One dilemma is the choice between efficiency and extravagance in the design of institutions and policies. One of the distinctive features of modern-day Western thinking about public administration is that we often do not recognize this as a choice at all. For the past forty years, research and practice in public administration have focused on providing high-quality services at the lowest possible cost. Efficiency has been the main concern of the public management movement that emerged in the 1970s and now dominates the field of public administration in the West. The goal is to make government "work better and cost less" and to increase "value for money."[1] In this view, organizations are healthy if they are lean and performance-focused. Wastefulness and extravagance are regarded as cardinal sins.

This emphasis on efficiency and disdain for waste makes sense, given the circumstances in which the public management movement emerged. After the 1970s, many governments in the developed world encountered serious budget problems. Spending increased while economic growth and tax revenues stagnated: the results were chronic budget deficits and mounting public debt. People were angry about attempts to reduce deficits by raising taxes or cutting services. It was tempting for leaders to argue that the real problem in government was wastefulness, because this meant budget deficits could be slashed without tax hikes or service reductions. Thus efficiency became the mantra. Throughout the West, there was an "obsession . . . with reduced-cost public service delivery."[2]

In Western politics today, efficiency and legitimacy seem to be inextricably connected. Leaders believe that they will only regain public trust if they work frugally. This might also seem to be the lesson of history. After all, the United States was formed out of a rebellion against high taxes. Leaders who have behaved with too much ostentation, whose administrations took on the trappings of royal courts, have been mocked and turned out of office. In the Progressive Era, advocates of good government also preached the "gospel of efficiency," calling on leaders to purge waste, corruption, and extravagance.[3]

But the choice between efficiency and extravagance is not so clear. Sometimes it makes sense to apply more resources to a task than is strictly necessary to accomplish it. For example, this is often true when fighting wars. In the early 1990s, just as "doing more with less" became the refrain in domestic policy, the U.S. government adopted the Powell Doctrine for military affairs. Articulated by General Colin Powell, chairman of the U.S. Joint Chiefs of Staff, the doctrine said that military objectives should be defined narrowly and that force should be applied in an overwhelming manner.[4] This meant doing less with more, not more with less. The Powell Doctrine was a reaction to the debacle in Vietnam, a war fought in an era when benefit-cost analysis was rigorously applied to military affairs and the goal of U.S. policy was wielding "the needed amount of effective military power at minimum cost."[5]

But the Vietnam-era focus on efficiency was an aberration in the domain of military affairs. The importance of overwhelming force has been long established among military strategists. Sometimes, the consequences of defeat are so dire that it is better to err on the side of caution when preparing for battle. There are also symbolic advantages. Just the sight of overwhelming force might break the spirit of opponents and cause surrender. This is the principle of "shock and awe," also popularized in the 1990s: the theatrical application of massive power to "paralyze or so overload an adversary's perceptions . . . [that they are] rendered totally impotent."[6] Again, this is an argument for extravagance rather than efficiency.

The logic of shock and awe applies to the maintenance of internal order as well as the conduct of foreign wars. In fragile states, skimping in the deployment of security forces can undermine peace by encouraging challenges to public authority. To rebels or criminals, the use of minimal force may signal a lack of political will or capacity to impose order. Sometimes the better course for leaders is ostentation, a "show of force . . . to demonstrate commitment or intimidate enemies."[7] President George Washington gathered a force of thirteen thousand men to put down a tax rebellion in Pennsylvania in 1794, not because this was the number actually required to restore authority, but because it would "overawe the disaffected individuals."[8] At the start of the twentieth century, American governments refined tactics for large urban strikes and protests that followed Washington's example.[9] It was believed that "energetic intervention" would reduce the "potentialities for violence."[10] The same logic motivated the deployment of troops in the American capital and other cities in the 1960s and the response to anti-globalization protests in the late 1990s.[11] Maintaining order was understood to require bold action. In 2017, top officers in the Los Angeles Police Department explained how they would avoid a repeat of that city's devastating 1992 riots: LAPD would "flood the zone," they explained, using "overwhelming strength to put down the riots in the early stages, preventing them from spreading."[12]

There are other ways that government behavior is driven by extravagance rather than efficiency. We see it in the design and location of government buildings, especially those built when state authority is in doubt. "The keeping up of an outward appearance of power," a British bureaucrat wrote in 1811, while explaining the design of imperial offices in India, "will in many instances save the necessity of resort into the actual exercise of it."[13] Leaders in democratic regimes have also used architecture "to seduce, to impress, and to intimidate."[14] In the early years of the American republic, the preferred architectural style was drawn from ancient Greece and Rome: even though it was impractical, the style conveyed solidity and a commitment to republican principles. The new American capital was set up as a field of monumental neoclassical structures. In the decades after the strife of the Civil War, there was another boom in public construction, this time in the equally impractical Beaux Arts style. Intended to cultivate civic and national pride, these buildings were typically described as imposing, splendid, impressive, and grand.[15] One of these was the State, War, and Navy building, now the Eisenhower Executive Office Building, adjacent to the White House, which was celebrated in the 1880s as "the finest building in Washington."[16] The Great Depression of the 1930s produced yet another style, WPA Moderne, a streamlined monumentalism designed to elicit feelings of security and confidence in the depths of the Depression.[17]

Often, deliberate inefficiency in the design of government programs is justified by concern for the symbolic effect of public action. In the nineteenth century, when the American border was still rolling westward, the federal government maintained a network of frontier outposts that were small and widely dispersed. These outposts were difficult to maintain and arguably ineffective from the point of view of deploying force. But they showed the flag: simply by their presence, they expressed the U.S. claim to the borderlands. Similar considerations affected the development of the postal service. The U.S. government set up routes and post offices in rural and frontier areas that were uneconomical but made the presence of the federal government known.[18] In the late nineteenth and early twentieth centuries, governments also located armories in expensive downtown locations because the buildings expressed a claim to territory. They showed the flag, just as frontier outposts did.

Deliberate wastefulness is not always about showing the flag. Sometimes, the goal is exactly the opposite: to obscure the reality of governmental action. Many federal programs depend on the joint effort of federal, state, and local government agencies as well as private contractors and voluntary organizations. It is much harder to coordinate action and maintain a focus on performance in these extensive "multi-sector service delivery networks." Resources are burned up as managers try to make all of the pieces fit together. Still, this waste is tolerated because the design has certain political advantages. One is that the reality of large-scale federal action is obscured. Americans have big government without seeing it and, consequently, without fighting over it. The "submerged state," as Suzanne Mettler calls it, "renders the electorate oblivious and passive."[19]

One might argue that the tension between efficiency and extravagance does not really exist. Leaders who spend more money than strictly necessary—on shows of force, architectural ostentation, services in remote locations, or complex program designs—often know what they are doing. They are attending to some of the fundamental concerns of government, like establishing authority, keeping the peace, and maintaining legitimacy. When we look at the goals articulated in government reports for some public programs—delivering the mail, providing healthcare, running courts or national parks—these more fundamental concerns might not be explicitly acknowledged. As a result, aspects of program design that address those concerns might not be appreciated. Thus the programs may seem to be structured in ways that are wasteful. But there might still be a kind of efficiency when these more fundamental considerations are taken into account.

And conditions may simply evolve, so that fundamental goals like establishing authority are no longer priorities. In the nineteenth century, the capacity of the U.S. federal government to exercise effective control over its territory was in doubt, and it made sense to spend liberally to affirm that control. By contrast, effective control over territory was largely established in the late twentieth century—except in some urban areas, where old ideas about showing the flag and flooding the zone still influenced strategies of urban policing. Efficiency was emphasized in other spheres of domestic policy because, in the unusual circumstances of mature democracies at the turn of the millennium, that seemed like the most effective way of restoring trust. This might have been the right choice in that time and place—but the emphasis on efficiency was nonetheless a choice and not a given.[20]

Chapter 15

Tight or Loose Control

A second dilemma in the design of governance strategies relates to strictness of control. Leaders must choose whether to monitor and regulate behavior loosely or intensively. This is certainly true with regard to control of the everyday conduct of citizens through surveillance and policing. A similar choice must be made in the economic sphere, between a command economy and free markets. And the dilemma arises again within the apparatus of the state itself. For example, central government must decide whether to exercise more or less supervision over lower levels of government. And within each level of government, political leaders must decide whether to give more or less autonomy to bureaucrats charged with implementing their policies. In all of these contexts, similar calculations about the right measure of control must be made.

Sometimes leaders dispute that they have freedom to make choices about retaining or giving away control. A person swimming against a strong current works hard just to avoid being swept away. Similarly, some leaders focus mainly on retaining control, believing their efforts are undermined constantly by countervailing forces. A situation in which leaders exercise too much control seems to them to be largely hypothetical. In their view, the battle is to resist entropy and keep an adequate grip on public affairs.

This viewpoint is self-serving but should not be dismissed immediately. Most countries in the world can be counted as fragile states, in which effective control over territory and people is barely established and in which there may be pockets of territory where control is not established at all. In these countries, there is rudimentary capacity for monitoring what the population is doing and for shaping its behavior. In this context, a single-minded concern with reinforcing control might be understandable. Even in developed countries, governments struggle to maintain their control capabilities. In the United States, for example, there have been intense political assaults on administrative agencies that collect statistics (such as the Bureau of Labor Statistics or the Census Bureau) essential to control and on agencies like the Environmental Protection Agency or the Occupational Safety and Health Administration that regulate behavior. Despite an extensive bureaucracy, noncompliance and evasion of the law continue to be widespread problems in the United States. Some experts on policy implementation in the United States are skeptical about the likely effectiveness of any policy that requires Americans to act against their beliefs or self-interest.[1]

National leaders felt especially beleaguered in the 1990s. Academic literature about the "end of the nation-state" emphasized how they had lost influence over their populations and economies.[2] The notion that leaders exercised significant influence over public affairs was described as a "nostalgic fiction."[3] This loss of control was blamed partly on technological advances that improved the ability of people and businesses to evade surveillance and regulation by national governments. Intellectual shifts over the last half century also undercut efforts to maintain central authority. The spread of "human rights thinking" made it harder for leaders to dictate the behavior of people; the diffusion of free market dogma made it harder to defend the detailed regulation of businesses; and doctrines of regional self-determination and subsidiarity made it harder to justify tight control of lower levels of government.

Still, national leaders do not deserve too much sympathy. The world is not conspiring against them entirely. There are ways in which long-term trends actually favor the extension of control. Before the early twentieth century, leaders at the center of government were forced to delegate authority to subordinates because it took so long for messages to shuttle to and from remote outposts. Today, it is easier to monitor the actions of subordinates and issue immediate instructions. Similarly, it is technically easier to intercept the everyday communications of citizens. Electoral dynamics and changes in the media also make it easier for central authorities to justify expansion of their responsibilities. In the United States, competition for middle-class votes has increased the federal role in education and healthcare, which are traditionally state and local responsibilities. Meanwhile, nonstop national media coverage of natural disasters and terrorist attacks has encouraged a larger federal role in emergency response and internal security.

In fact, leaders do have substantial discretion over the level of control they choose to exercise. This is evidenced by the large variation in governance strategies pursued by states. Freedom House, a non-governmental organization, produces an annual ranking that shows wide divergences in respect to human rights.[4] The daily life of people in Saudi Arabia is regulated more strictly than in Australia. Similarly, the Fraser Institute finds that countries differ substantially in their attitudes toward control of the economic sphere: Switzerland is much more tolerant of free markets than Brazil.[5] Measures of decentralization—the extent to which people at the apex of government share power with those further down—also reveal large differences among states. In some countries, the autonomy of regions and localities is guaranteed in constitutions, while in others, power is closely held at the center.[6]

The United States is usually identified as one of those countries that tilt toward loose control. Governance strategies crafted by American leaders since the Revolution have tended to favor civil liberties, free markets, states' rights, and home rule. Still, there has been significant variation over time. Understandings about the boundaries of individual freedom have generally broadened, although security crises have often induced setbacks, and advances for African Americans and other minorities have been slow and uneven. Governments have also experimented with intensive economic controls—tariffs, wage and price restrictions, industrial subsidies, rationing, and even outright ownership of industrial enterprises—especially during times of economic crisis and war. Respect for states' rights has oscillated as well. There is also significant variation among the fifty states in respect to civil rights, the extent of economic regulation, and the autonomy given to city governments.

Considerations of principle often weigh in favor of loose control. The ultimate goal of state action is to advance human welfare, and this cannot be accomplished without creating a zone within which individuals are free to shape their own lives. Our understanding of how big that zone should be is constantly evolving.[7] Decisions to forbear from economic regulation can also be justified on the grounds that the marketplace is a forum for the expression of human creativity as well as a mechanism for the production of essential goods and services. The devolution of authority to lower levels of government can be defended in the language of individual rights as well, if those lower levels are more likely to be accountable to citizens. However, there is no necessary equation between respect for human rights and free market policies or devolution to state and local governments. Market interventions might be necessary to correct gross inequalities among citizens, and central government action might be necessary to stop human-rights abuses by lower tiers of government. The politics of the Progressive Era was concerned with the expansion of central control over markets to defend the "rights of workingmen," just as the expansion of central control over state governments in the 1950s–1960s was justified as a way of protecting the civil rights of African Americans.

Necessity influences decisions about the extent of control as well. In wartime, when the survival of the state is in doubt, governments often restrict civil liberties and intervene more directly in the economy. During World War I, and briefly during World War II, the U.S. government actually took charge of the railroad industry, which was the critical component of the country's transportation and communications infrastructure. Internal emergencies have also resulted in tightened control; for example, through the imposition of military government in riotous cities—a common phenomenon throughout American history—and the use of military force to stop secession and restore order after the Civil War. The Great Depression was also viewed as a national emergency that justified President Franklin Roosevelt's reach for warlike powers. President George W. Bush made a similar bid for authority during the financial crisis of 2008. And in 2016, many Americans voted for Donald Trump because he promised to be a strong leader who would resolve a crisis of broken and dysfunctional government in Washington.

On the other hand, tightening control might not always be the best response to an emergency. Centralization of authority allows decisive action in critical moments but creates vulnerability if the center becomes incapable of decision-making—if it is overloaded, gridlocked, or otherwise incapacitated. Another way to promote societal resilience is by creating a network of relatively autonomous power centers that can survive even if one or more of those centers is crippled. Decentralization also makes sense when there is uncertainty about how to handle new circumstances, because it allows societies to explore a broader range of responses. This is what Louis Brandeis had in mind in 1932 when he famously described American states as laboratories for "social and economic experiments . . . [in] remolding institutions to meet changing needs."[8]

Available capacity affects choices about control too. Central authorities cannot assert authority if they lack the administrative capabilities necessary to make rules, monitor compliance with those rules, and punish noncompliance. If leaders impose rules but seem incapable of enforcing them, their credibility can be badly damaged. And there are other practical considerations. There are limits to the number of issues that central authorities can handle competently at one time. A study of presidential advisors in the 1970s found that they were "overwhelmed with operational stuff": exhausted and lacking time to think problems through, presidential staff focused on "quick fixes" and "putting out fires."[9] The situation has not improved over the following forty years.

Centralization can also aggravate sectional or factional tensions if there are sharp disagreements about what the substance of centrally dictated policy should be. With loose control, sections that have divergent preferences can agree to disagree. Moreover, ordinary citizens can grow tired of tight control. People make sacrifices in moments of emergency, but the spirit of sacrifice usually dissipates when the emergency is over. At that point, leaders start to wear down the goodwill of the population. This suggests that there is also an important temporal tradeoff in choices about control. Tightening the reins might be expedient today, but it might undermine the legitimacy necessary to exert control tomorrow. I look at temporal tradeoffs more closely in chapter 17.

Chapter 16

Separation or Connection

"If we don't have borders," presidential candidate Donald Trump said in 2016, "we don't have a country." Going by the plain meaning of Trump's words, it is hard to disagree. States are created when leaders draw a line around territory and achieve effective control within that line. Territory is divided from the rest of the world by the act of statemaking. But leaders can choose to take borders more or less seriously. The boundary lines of a state may be impermeable or permeable. Borders may allow for greater or lesser flows of people, information, money, and goods. They may be seen as walls that shelter distinctive ways of life or as administrative conveniences set up to govern people who are basically the same on either side.

When leaders devise governance strategies, they must decide whether borders will emphasize separation or connection with the rest of the world—yet another dilemma in the design of governance strategies. Such a decision is not easy, and different considerations—national security, economic growth, internal cohesion, human rights—may pull in opposite directions.

In the early years of the republic, American leaders often emphasized separation from the rest of the world. The United States was a new and fragile state, at risk of being crushed in the struggle among the great powers of Europe. Presidents Washington and Jefferson warned against entangling the United States in European affairs.[1] The United States would rely on the vast Atlantic Ocean for its protection. "The policy of the Americans in relation to the whole world is exceedingly simple," Alexis de Tocqueville wrote in 1835. "It may almost be said that no country stands in need of them, nor do they require the co-operation of any other people."[2] One senator explained in 1851 that American policy was to "mind its own business and let the business of other people alone."[3] Forty years later, a respected scholar could still observe that America "stands apart in a world apart . . . [and] has little occasion to think of foreign affairs."[4]

The extent of American isolation in the nineteenth century can be exaggerated. The United States fought Mediterranean pirates, waged a war with Mexico that resulted in the acquisition of a half million square miles of territory, and sent gunboats to open new markets in China and Japan. The Monroe Doctrine, which demanded that European powers stop meddling in the New World, relied on a tacit alliance with the United Kingdom, whose navy enforced the American edict.[5]

American prosperity also depended on commercial and financial connections with the United Kingdom. After the War of 1812 and until the Civil War, the American and British economies were indivisible. The United States sent millions of bales of cotton to the United Kingdom and, in exchange, received vast amounts of capital and manufactured goods. Even in the era of globalization that began in the 1990s, the American economy was not as open as it had been in the decades before the Civil War.[6] Many American leaders were uneasy about this fact. Some were humiliated by dependence on Britain, saying that it compromised the country's ability to challenge British claims to territory on its northern and western frontiers. And it made American prosperity vulnerable to upsets in the British economy. To truly achieve security and prosperity, it seemed that the United States needed economic self-sufficiency, especially in industrial production.

In the eighty years following the Civil War, America's policy regarding engagement with the world turned upside down. In fits and starts, the United States abandoned its policy of military and diplomatic isolation. By 1900, it had colonized the Philippines, one of the most populous lands in Asia. By

1945, it had built up the most powerful military force in the world, and American diplomats had brokered the end of two world wars. The United States was on its way to becoming "the world's government."[7] But economic policy often emphasized separation rather integration. In some ways, economic exchanges with the rest of the world were regulated more strictly than they had been in much of the nineteenth century. For example, the Great Depression of the 1930s led to tight controls on the exchange of capital across borders, while tariffs continued to discourage the inflow of foreign goods. An important exception to the drive for economic independence was the overseas search for energy. After the 1950s, the United States was burning more oil than it was pumping from the earth. Economic necessity led to military and diplomatic entanglement in the oil-rich Middle East.

In the late twentieth century, attitudes about foreign policy shifted again. For a moment, the end of the Cold War seemed to signal a retreat from military and diplomatic engagement. But this retreat was halted after the resurgence of international terrorism in the early 2000s. At the same time, American leaders abandoned many restrictions on international trade and finance so that economic integration with the rest of the world deepened. For the first time, security and economic considerations seemed to be pushing in the same direction. Experts and politicians celebrated the advent of a "borderless world."[8] Of course, this was hyperbole: nobody advocated the outright elimination of borders. Rather, they argued that borders were less consequential. Populist leaders like Donald Trump rebelled against this attitude after the financial crisis of 2007–2008. Trump advocated for a return to diplomatic isolation and economic self-sufficiency.

The significance of borders is not shaped only by concerns about national security and prosperity. Considerations of internal order and cohesion come into play. For most of the nineteenth century, there were few restrictions on immigration to the United States: people could disembark at New York or New Orleans and wander freely across American territory. Immigrants were needed to consolidate American control of western territories and stoke the American economy. But surges in immigration often caused internal disorder. The rush of Irish immigrants into eastern seaports in the 1840s triggered political upheaval, as newcomers and natives fought over jobs and over control of schools, police, and other public institutions. The doctrine of nativism—the belief that immigrants of the wrong kind endangered the American system—took root.[9] The doctrine was revived in response to the influx of Chinese workers on the West Coast later in the nineteenth century, eastern Europeans on the East Coast in the early twentieth century, and Mexicans in the southwest after the 1970s. Each rush of immigration provoked countermeasures to defend "American values and institutions."

Openness can also undermine internal cohesion by dividing elites and masses. In the nineteenth century, national politics was dominated by an Eastern elite with close cultural and economic ties to Britain. In moments of crisis, ordinary people often challenged the loyalties of the elite, alleging that they were Anglophiles rather than American patriots. Senator Joseph McCarthy's anti-elite crusade after World War II was driven by the same suspicion of disloyalty: many statesmen and bureaucrats were "internationalists" or "one-worlders," McCarthy said, and not true Americans. This split reappeared as globalization intensified at the end of the twentieth century. In 2004, Samuel Huntington saw a "major gap" between the country's cosmopolitan elite and its "'Thank God for America' public."[10] Sometimes this elite was called the "Davos crowd," because many of its members congregated at annual meetings held by the World Economic Forum in Davos, Switzerland. The Davos crowd was convinced that globalization was the key to universal prosperity; however, their celebration of globalization weakened their hold on power at home. The election of Donald Trump was widely interpreted as a rejection of government by "the party of Davos."[11]

In the twenty-first century, there are good reasons why American leaders must look beyond their borders. Some dangers—climate change, nuclear proliferation, terrorism, economic instability—can be addressed properly only by building international institutions that promote cooperation among states. The challenge for leaders is to build these institutions without appearing to betray people back home. The doctrine of universal human rights, consolidated over the last seventy years, complicates strategy-making even further, because it sometimes demands that foreigners be given treatment comparable to that of citizens. But this doctrine might not be well understood or generally accepted by many people within the United States. Michael Ignatieff has recently suggested that it might just be "the lingua franca of an influential but thinly spread stratum" of the world's population.[12] Many Americans still hew to the older view that rights are a product of "common citizenship"—that is, common to those people who are sheltered behind borders.

Chapter 17

Present or Future

When they wrestle over separation or connection with the rest of the world, leaders struggle with a geographical frontier. They decide how much a line on the ground will matter. At the same time, leaders also think about another border as they formulate a strategy for governing. This is the temporal divide between present and future, the invisible line that separates the present generation from the generations that follow. Institutions can be designed to give more weight to the interests of future generations. But leaders are often reluctant to do this, because they must also respond to more immediate challenges.

People are reasonably good at thinking about the future if they know that the welfare of their children is at stake. For example, parents are usually happy to invest in the education of their offspring. But people are worse at handling problems that will affect people they do not know many decades from now. For example, engineers warn about a looming infrastructure crisis in the United States, caused by the refusal to maintain roads, water and sewer systems, and public buildings. Why would we shortchange maintenance, given that we can foresee the likely consequences? Because we save a few dollars today, the harm will not be realized until much later, and it will be suffered by strangers. Similarly, experts warn of a budget crisis caused by our habit of borrowing to pay for current government expenditures. We are said to be mortgaging the future. And perhaps the most frightening example of shortsightedness is the problem of climate change. For decades, the world has been burning more oil, gas, and coal, despite mounting evidence that this damages the planet's capacity to support life. Pessimists look at the historical record and argue that civilizations often destroy the environments on which they depend.[1] They worry that we are in the process of doing this on a global scale.

But governments are not always shortsighted. In some areas, they are reasonably good at thinking about the future. In the United States, the Department of Defense regularly reviews threats to national security that will likely face the next generation. These reviews range broadly: the last assessment, completed in 2014, even acknowledged the danger that climate change would "devastate homes, land, and infrastructure."[2] Military planners also oversee research and development projects that span decades: for example, it took a quarter of a century to design and deploy the sophisticated F-22 fighter aircraft. Skeptics say that this sort of forward planning serves the interests of the defense bureaucracy, by stoking fear about national security and thus protecting its pet programs. A counterargument is that the bureaucratic self-regard has been enlisted as a check against shortsightedness on matters of national security. Leaders have built institutions with a vested interest in tending to future threats.

In fact, leaders constantly tinker with institutions in an attempt to cure shortsightedness.[3] Sometimes they set up autonomous agencies with taxing powers to make sure that critical assets, such as airports or highways, are properly maintained. Similarly, independent trustees for the U.S. Social Security program are charged with publishing estimates of its expenditures seventy-five years into the future. In the 1980s, as concern about indebtedness grew, Congress mandated the production of thirty-year budget forecasts and adopted balanced-budget laws intended to curb borrowing. With American support, the International Monetary Fund also increased scrutiny of the budget policies of the 189 member countries of that international organization, to encourage long-term responsibility. We learned about climate change mainly because governments worked together to support research in the 1980s and 1990s. Governments have also signed treaties and set up international organizations in an attempt to discourage the burning of oil, gas, and coal. Some national governments have even created independent organizations whose job is to warn against any policies that seem likely to harm future generations.[4]

Granted, these institutional checks against myopia are frequently weak and ineffectual. Sometimes leaders are distracted by the need to maintain internal legitimacy. In democratic systems, people are given the right to select leaders in exchange for their support of the regime. But voters seem to favor themselves at the expense of future generations. "Democracy is always short-sighted and selfish," a nineteenth-century writer lamented.[5] Conservatives in the United States made the same complaint in the 1960s and 1970s: that voters were overloading the government with demands for new benefits while refusing to pay taxes, so leaders were forced to take on debt.

Some environmentalists also blame selfish voters for the failure to take climate change seriously. They argue that some form of well-intentioned authoritarianism—a "green dictatorship"—may be the only way to avoid catastrophe.[6] It is not clear, however, that this prescription would make much of a difference. Even authoritarian regimes need to maintain the support of the population. Chinese leaders, for example, worry constantly about protests and social instability. They try to appease the people with rapid economic growth. But rapid growth also means burning more oil, gas, and coal. Chinese leaders may not face elections, but they are not exempt from the realities of everyday governance. Their economic policies have made China the leading generator of emissions that contribute to global warming.

Sometimes external factors also drive leaders toward shortsightedness. Any state, democratic or authoritarian, must deal with the reality of competition within the system of states. To maintain security and influence, leaders must keep their national economies growing, even if it causes long-term environmental damage. A bigger economy means more tax revenue to pay for armed forces and aid to allies. Domestic prosperity also makes it easier to negotiate trade agreements, because other countries want access to well-heeled consumers. National leaders might be willing to refrain from this sort of destructive competition if they could be sure that other states would also restrain themselves. But it is difficult to achieve this result. The incentives for states to renege on promises of restraint are strong, and there is no supreme authority to punish promise-breakers. Negotiations on climate change have been drawn out while diplomats hunt for clever ways to identify and shame countries that renege on their commitments.

Shortsightedness is not just the result of skewed incentives and flawed institutions. It is also the result of flawed ideas, a defect in our moral imagination. For centuries, Western intellectuals have emphasized two related ideas: liberation and dominion. For Enlightenment thinkers, liberation meant freeing people from the dead hand of the past. "The earth belongs always to the living generation," Thomas Jefferson insisted in 1789. "They may manage it ... as they please."[7] Dominion meant increasing humanity's capacity to conquer and subdue nature, to make it a slave to human ends, as Francis Bacon said in the seventeenth century.[8] Four centuries ago, human influence over nature was so modest that it is difficult to see how the drive to enslave nature could jeopardize the welfare of future generations.

Only in the last two generations have we begun to seriously question this drive for liberation and dominion. Since the 1960s, understanding about the environmental costs of economic development has improved. More people are aware that there are limits to growth, even if they disagree about where those limits are. The notion that development ought to be sustainable has gained a foothold. Similarly, people are more likely to acknowledge that future generations also have rights that need to be respected. The shift in attitudes seems slow—and this is understandable, given that it results partly from the displacement of one generation by the next. Still, this change in thinking has made it easier for leaders to experiment with institutional innovations that correct myopia in environmental policy.

In fact, there is evidence that this shift in attitudes and policies is happening faster in democracies than in authoritarian states.[9] This is not just because people in established democracies are better educated and wealthier, enabling them to afford to make sacrifices on behalf of future generations. Even in India (a democracy), people worry more about climate change than people in China (a one-party state), according to opinion polls. In free societies, it is easier to exchange information about looming threats, organize with like-minded people, and lobby government to change policies. The overall tendency of democracies may still be toward shortsightedness, but there is a capacity for learning and innovation that is suppressed in authoritarian regimes. This is another pragmatic reason why leaders might favor democracy, even if it jeopardizes their survival in office. We already know that democratic systems may be useful for bolstering internal legitimacy and protecting human rights. But they might also improve the capacity of the state to reconfigure itself—that is, to adapt and survive.

Chapter 18

Commitment or Equivocation

For the last thirty years, "credible commitment" has been a stock phrase in scholarly writing about government. Governments are said to have a credibility problem, because citizens and businesses do not trust them to keep promises about how they will behave in the future. Public institutions are thought to be fickle and unreliable. The task for leaders is to find techniques for demonstrating that they will keep their word, by designing institutions that make it hard to break promises. These institutional arrangements are called commitment devices.

Many economists believe that credible commitment is essential to economic development. For example, people are unlikely to improve their property if they believe that leaders might seize it later on. Laws that restrict the power to take property, along with independent courts to enforce those laws, reassure property owners that it is safe to make improvements. Laws protecting property rights and independent courts are commitment devices, and leaders may find it advantageous to adopt them to spur growth, even though these devices limit their own power.[1] Similarly, leaders can adopt laws that constrain their ability to influence a country's central bank, as a way of showing investors that they are committed to a stable currency. Central bank independence is also a commitment device.[2] So is a legal guarantee of independence for regulatory agencies, because it assures investors that regulations will not be changed arbitrarily.[3] And constitutional restrictions on government borrowing provide a credible commitment that governments will not spend recklessly.[4] The idea that leaders could promote prosperity by adopting such constraints and creating a "stable environment for business" was very popular in the 1990s. Thomas Friedman said that leaders were donning a "golden straitjacket."[5]

Commitment devices are used for other purposes too. In war-torn states, opposing forces have a commitment problem: neither side wants to put down its guns until it is sure that the other side will disarm as well. An outside force can act as a commitment device by guaranteeing that the terms of peace will be respected.[6] At the same time, constitutions can be written to reassure rival factions that power will be shared and autonomy will be respected: the drafting of the American Constitution was partly a project of inventing clever commitment devices to maintain internal peace.[7] And to build trust among the general public, leaders can delegate power to a professional bureaucracy, constitutionalize fundamental rights, adopt open government laws, and take other steps to guarantee impartial treatment.[8] Many countries try to reassure voters about the fairness of elections by handing over that function to independent electoral commissions.[9]

We might conclude from all of this that leaders are mainly concerned with finding clever ways to solve commitment problems. Commitment, it seems, is the key to prosperity, order, and legitimacy. Leaders want people and businesses to make choices that stimulate growth and deepen their own attachment to the existing order. And leaders want to build something that testifies to their greatness—something durable and consequential.

But the situation confronting leaders is actually more difficult than this. Sometimes equivocation rather than commitment is the sound choice. Leaders know that there will inevitably be emergencies where everyday rules have to be put aside, and they do not want to make it impossible to do this. For example, property might need to be seized in the name of national defense. There are other ways in which the public welfare could be improved by breaking promises to individuals—by taking land for a new highway, for example. In addition, there are times when leaders are grappling with uncertainty and experimenting with policies, and they want to preserve the discretion to abandon policies that prove ineffective. Similarly, leaders may want to discourage attachment to policies that will become obsolete because of rapidly changing conditions. And sometimes overt commitments inflame factional conflicts rather than subdue them. In antebellum America, national leaders could not make clear commitments to slave states without enraging free states, and vice versa. Vagueness about the direction of future policy was a technique for avoiding civil war.

There are other tensions. For example, the drive for commitment in the name of economic development may undermine other national goals. On one hand, businesspeople like stability in political leadership and policies. They like to know who they will do business with and that the rules of the game will not change. On the other hand, democracy requires that people be allowed to change rulers and laws, which necessarily undermines the ability of leaders to make commitments. "One of the principal vices of the elective system," de Tocqueville observed in 1835, "is that it always introduces a certain degree of instability into the internal and external policy of the State."[10] There are ways to adjust voting rules and other laws to reduce instability, but instability cannot be eliminated. Democratic rule inevitably collides with the predictability of economic policies.

Leaders must make difficult choices about whether and how to "lock in" policies by the use of commitment devices. One predicament arises when leaders want to build a reputation for constancy, but are not quite sure about the wisdom of a particular policy in the long run. The challenge in that case is to make a show of commitment while actually preserving discretion. Another predicament arises when ordinary people run ahead of leaders and "lock in" to policies prematurely. They acquire a vested interest in the status quo, which makes it difficult for leaders to adjust when circumstances change. Scholars who write about path dependence in public policy or sclerosis in government are worried about this second predicament.[11]

These two predicaments may be handled in different ways. To build a reputation for constancy while preserving discretion, leaders may deploy commitment devices that still leave room for maneuver. In the 1980s and 1990s, American politicians resisted an amendment to the U.S. Constitution that would have required a balanced budget, relying instead on ordinary legislation that could be adjusted when the economy slowed down or politics became fractious. Similarly, constitutional and legislative protections for private property have been crafted so that policymakers still have the capacity to expropriate property for public purposes and to do so quickly when emergencies arise. Leaders may also rely on informal arrangements to qualify their formal commitments. For example, agencies or courts may appear to be independent, but leaders find the right kind of people to lead them and develop private routines for coordination. And leaders may use rhetoric to make their commitments seem more robust than they actually are. In the extreme, they may simply lie about what they intend to do.[12]

The second predicament—discouraging people from becoming prematurely committed to policies—may be handled differently. Sometimes policies are explicitly announced as temporary measures or experiments so that people do not become unduly attached to them. Legislators may append "sunset clauses" to new laws so that they become invalid after a specified date. Responsibility for short-term measures may be given to new agencies that have no strong constituencies rather than to established agencies that are better able to resist policy reversals. Finally, leaders can impose conditions that diminish the survival prospects for a policy—such as requirements to disclose internal information about policy development and implementation, to undergo periodic evaluation, or to accept supervision by skeptical outsiders.

It is hard to craft policies that strike the right balance between commitment and equivocation. Laws that promise commitment but preserve discretion are often condemned as shams. Balanced-budget laws adopted in the 1980s and 1990s were derided because Congress retained the power to change them. Similarly, critics have questioned whether the Federal Reserve, the nation's central bank, is really free of political influence. At the same time, devices designed to avoid premature commitment are said to be ineffectual: sometimes sunset clauses and other checks are overwhelmed by the power of vested interests, so that temporary measures become permanent fixtures.

In many cases, though, such criticisms are overwrought. Muddy compromises that try to reconcile commitment and equivocation are never satisfying to purists, and they do sometimes fail. Often, though, they are effective in accomplishing their conflicting purposes. They provide the measure of commitment needed to promote growth and security but also give leaders the discretion to manage factionalism, uncertainty, and turbulence.

Chapter 19

Planning or Improvisation

Who could be opposed to planning? The world is a chaotic, sometimes dangerous place. Surely it makes sense to identify current and future threats, prepare for contingencies, coordinate effort, and use scarce resources wisely. "To plan or not to plan is no real issue," Charles Merriam wrote in 1944. "The only issue is who shall plan for what ends."[1] Merriam was a member of the United States' first national planning board, established by President Roosevelt in 1939.[2] But Merriam was wrong about the real issue. The choice is not binary: plan or no plan. Plans may be more or less comprehensive and more or less detailed. A broadly stated short-term plan is different from a highly regimented long-term plan. The question is not just who shall plan for what ends but also how broad and detailed plans should be.

Enthusiasm for large-scale planning—also known as overall, comprehensive, long-term, economic, or social planning—boomed and collapsed in twentieth century. At the start of that century, progressive reformers seized on planning as the remedy for the United States' social and economic woes. Powerful forces wrenched the country at that time—industrialization, urbanization, mass migration, and rapid technological change—and a feeling that the country was coming unglued was widely felt. Government seemed ramshackle and impotent. Careful planning, guided by experts, would be the device by which internal order was restored. "Civilization," Walter Lippmann said in 1914, "is just this constant effort to introduce plan where there has been clash, and purpose into the jungles of disordered growth."[3]

Fear of internal disorder abated in the prosperous 1920s but returned more fiercely during the economic crisis of the 1930s. Experts became convinced that capitalism was a dangerously unstable system of economic production and that it had to be disciplined as a matter of public safety.[4] A "comprehensive national plan" was their preferred instrument for doing this. Meanwhile voters demanded that leaders present a clear program for resolving the crisis. During the presidential election of 1932, Franklin Roosevelt assured voters that he was a firm believer in national planning "for a long time to come."[5] Soon after his inauguration, Roosevelt set up agencies to guide overall planning. But none of this amounted to much, because Roosevelt was not a planner at heart. He was a pragmatist who disliked rigid schemes. Still, Roosevelt was savvy enough to know that voters wanted assurance and a sense of direction. He made a show of planning while pursuing a policy of improvisation.

The pressures of foreign affairs also encouraged interest in planning in the United States in the 1920s and 1930s. The international order was unstable in the period between the two world wars. Three countries—the Soviet Union, Italy, and Germany—appeared to be increasing their power as a consequence of careful central planning. The Soviet system of five-year plans, said *New York Times* journalist Walter Duranty, was "the biggest, boldest, newest thing in the whole wide world."[6] Fascist Italy and Germany, meanwhile, were admired for their determination to impose "conscious, intelligent ordering" on social and economic affairs.[7] Judgments about the actual effectiveness of these policies turned out to be misguided, but what matters are the perceptions of that time. Americans believed that they were being outpaced by rival states that took planning seriously. Even Roosevelt admired Mussolini in the early 1930s.

Two world wars hardened the belief that overall planning was not only desirable but feasible. These were *total wars*, to use a phrase that entered circulation in the 1930s: all-in struggles that required mobilization of all "productive forces of the nation" according to a "large scale government plan."[8]

The United States did this twice within a generation and emerged as a superpower as a consequence. After the war, defeated states had to be reconstructed, and this was also done according to large-scale plans. Similarly, the international order was carefully planned and rebuilt with the purpose of avoiding a relapse into war. Progressives wondered why the same methods could not be applied to domestic policy in peacetime. What was needed, William James observed at the dawn of the Progressive Era, was the "moral equivalent of war" in the realm of internal affairs: an assault on social problems conducted with the discipline and selflessness that typified military campaigns.[9]

The vogue for planning was buoyed by growing confidence among experts about their capacity to diagnose and treat social and economic problems. Graduate training and research in the social sciences expanded in the first half of the twentieth century, and knowledge about social and economic conditions improved considerably. By the 1960s, some social scientists had succumbed to overconfidence. Social problems that once seemed insoluble were now framed as merely technical difficulties that could be resolved by analysis and well-crafted interventions. The "unconditional war on poverty" declared by President Lyndon Johnson in 1964—the sort of intensive domestic campaign that William James had called for fifty years earlier—was launched because politicians and social scientists believed that they could invent an arsenal of programs that would make the war winnable. They had "faith in the ability to influence the future."[10]

The movement for overall social planning hit its zenith in the 1960s. This sort of planning was destined to increase in coming years, Alfred Kahn insisted in 1966. He echoed Merriam's words of 1944: "The critical questions are: who plans and how is it done?"[11] But Kahn, like Merriam, was mistaken. The truly critical question, it turned out, was whether planning could be done at all. By the end of the twentieth century, enthusiasm for large-scale planning had collapsed.

Planners of all kinds ran into three obstacles in the last quarter of the twentieth century. The first was popular resistance to the practice of planning. On one hand, people feared the social and economic disorder that planning was supposed to prevent. On the other hand, they disliked the centralization of authority and detailed regulation required by comprehensive planning. In the first half of the century, fear of disorder outweighed distaste for centralized power, but public attitudes shifted in the second half of the century. In the prosperous decades that followed World War II, fears about economic crisis dissipated. Meanwhile, hostility toward centralized power grew. As a result, planning schemes did not have the same positive effect on public opinion at the end of the twentieth century as at its start. In the 1930s, planning was a device for bolstering state legitimacy, but in the post-war period, planning tended to weaken it.

Allied to this fact was the reality that highly detailed plans were unworkable, in the sense that people could not always be compelled to do what the plans required. Individuals and companies found ways to evade requirements that were unduly burdensome, or they challenged those requirements in court and lobbied legislators to change the rules. This was what the current generation—the people whose own leaders had crafted the plan—could do. Future generations of leaders and citizens had even more freedom to ignore the plans passed down to them. They took seriously Jefferson's injunction that the earth belongs to the living. The implication was that planning would be impracticable beyond a decade or two: after that, all that one generation could do is offer advice to the next.

But the greatest obstacle to large-scale planning proved to be a failure of understanding. It turned out that social scientists had overestimated their ability to diagnose and cure economic and social problems. The easy confidence with which economists approached overall economic policy in the 1960s collapsed in the 1970s. Economic models were no longer useful in predicting the behavior of the system, and governmental interventions did not produce the expected results.[12] There was disillusionment in the domain of social policy as well. Many initiatives launched in the 1960s and early 1970s did not work as intended. A few social scientists had warned all along that the complexity of social and economic affairs was underestimated.[13] The implication of this was that government actions were likely to have unintended consequences. After the 1980s, this minority opinion hardened into conventional wisdom. It became known as the law of unintended consequences: "No matter what you think you're doing, the final result will be something different."[14]

This so-called law took hold within the social sciences almost as firmly as the idea of planning had fifty years earlier. It undermined faith in the possibility of planning. Plans could be made, but they were unlikely to be obeyed, and even if they were obeyed, they were unlikely to work as predicted. This conclusion fit well with the conservative drift in developed countries after the 1980s: it provided a practical reason for reducing the role of government. It was also deeply discouraging for people who cared about the future, because it implied that nothing could be done to address major social and economic ills.

But this was not the right conclusion. A better conclusion is that leaders should make plans while being realistic about the limits of planning. It is necessary to exercise foresight, set priorities, and design policies that seem likely to accomplish those priorities. Simply by doing this, leaders encourage coordination among individuals and businesses, through conversation about goals and tactics. Of course, leaders will go further by using incentives and commands to redirect effort. They must try to steer the ship. But the direction of the ship is not entirely under the captain's control, and eventually the captain, officers, and crew are all replaced. Leaders may decide that it is bad politics to acknowledge this point and perhaps even prudent to deny it, but there is a point beyond which the well-being of a state cannot be guaranteed through preventative action.

Neither is imperfect knowledge a total barrier to planning. There is no "law" of unintended consequences: it is not inevitable that government actions will produce entirely unexpected results. The more appropriate stance is modesty about what is known and what can be achieved. Plans that launch big schemes on brittle assumptions are more likely to fail. Plans that proceed more tentatively, that allow room for testing, learning, and adjustment, are less likely to collapse in the face of unexpected results.

This was the method that Franklin Roosevelt preferred, even as he talked about large-scale planning. "The country needs . . . bold, persistent experimentation," Roosevelt said in 1932. "It is common sense to take a method and try it: If it fails, admit it frankly and try another."[15] The dilemma for leaders, as Roosevelt recognized, is that the experimental method requires an admission of at least partial ignorance: we are not entirely sure what works and what does not. Such an admission may not always be good politics. Leaders must seem to have a hold on events even though, beyond a certain point, they do not. Leaders cannot direct the stream of time, German chancellor Otto von Bismarck said in the late nineteenth century; they only can sail on it with more or less skill.[16]

PART III

Applying the Approach

Chapter 20

Research

As the preceding pages suggest, there is no shortage of questions about strategies for governing: about how they are crafted, put into practice through institution-building and renovation, and adapted in response to changing circumstances. Some academics who are already engaged in public management research might object to pursuing these questions because they disagree about their importance. And some might object on a different basis: that even if the questions are important, there is no way of addressing them with rigor. To put it another way, the complaint is that there is no way to build reliable knowledge about strategies for governing.

This concern is foremost in the minds of many public management researchers. They are reacting against the indiscipline that seemed to characterize scholarship in public administration until the 1970s. Complaints about a lack of rigor in public administration research intensified in the 1980s.[1] "Lack of rigor" meant a failure to define concepts and problems precisely, to test the validity of claims properly, and to build on the work of earlier scholars. The entire discipline seemed like a sandcastle that collapsed as quickly as it was built. Some even dismissed the field of public administration as "a brain-dead endeavor."[2] Practical concerns about career advancement and status within academia stoked these concerns about lack of rigor. In the interdisciplinary schools of public policy established in the 1970s and 1980s, researchers in public management worked alongside scholars from "hard" disciplines such as economics, and struggled to win support from their peers when they applied for tenure and promotion.[3]

The public management approach was designed to overcome this stigma. Scholars in public management sought to focus on questions of manageable size, define concepts and hypotheses precisely, and rely on the quantitative-statistical research methods preferred by economists. All of this would assure "rigorous empirical analysis."[4] By the early 2000s, quantitative-statistical research methods were dominant in the field.[5] There was a general feeling that the weaknesses of public administration scholarship in the 1970s were being addressed seriously and that the field was on its way to becoming a real science.[6] The worry today is that a shift in the focus of research toward the macro-level of analysis—that is, toward big questions about the role and design of the state—will mean abandoning the accomplishments of the last thirty years. The field would no longer test precisely defined hypotheses using sophisticated methodologies and would revert to the loose, essayistic style that seemed to prevail before the 1980s.[7] Scholars would no longer be engaged in the project of building reliable, cumulative knowledge. And they would lose the respect of scholars in other disciplines as a result.

There are three ways to respond to such concerns. The first is to question whether the current strategy—focused on middle-level questions of management, using quantitative-statistical methods—really does produce a stockpile of reliable and useful knowledge. It is difficult to find overall appraisals of the accomplishments of the public management approach over the last forty years, and it is even more difficult to find studies that contrast the accomplishments of the public management approach with those of old-style public administration over the preceding forty years, from the 1930s to the 1970s.[8] Indeed, some recent scholarship has questioned the reliability of knowledge generated by public management scholars over the last four decades. Researchers have lamented the dearth of "replication investigations" that validate previously reported findings in the field.[9] They worry that researchers may be reporting results that are produced by chance or driven by unacknowledged contextual factors.[10] There is good reason to believe that such contextual factors are important, which suggests that the drive to focus on smaller and more tractable questions may have its limits. In the end, perhaps, the larger world cannot be shut out; the big picture cannot be ignored.

There is a second and more positive reply to methodological hardliners: that raising the level of analysis does not imply a loss of rigor. Concepts like the state can be defined with as much precision as many other concepts used within the public management approach—agency, performance, efficiency, and so on.[11] And researchers in other domains have shown that it is possible to apply quantitative-statistical research methods using state-level variables. At the same time, there have been significant advances in refining methods of qualitative research, so that hypotheses can be tested rigorously even where quantitative data is not available.[12]

Moreover, researchers have thrived in other domains even while pursuing high-level questions and applying qualitative methods. One example is in the field of scholarship dedicated to statebuilding, as noted in the introduction. Another is in the subdomain of political science known as American political development—essentially, statebuilding in the American context—which is roughly as old as the public management approach and has become one of the fastest-growing areas of research within American political science.[13] And the field of international relations has flourished even though a considerable amount of research in that field addresses big questions using qualitative methods.

I could say that these other fields have thrived even though they address big questions—but it would be more accurate to say that they have thrived *because* they address big and pressing questions. And this leads to the last and probably most important reply to methodological hardliners: the research agenda for public administration ought to be driven by the importance of questions and not by methodological preferences. If a question is urgent—if, for example, it relates to state survival or the capacity to perform essential tasks such as maintaining order and legitimacy—it should not be ignored simply because quantitative-statistical methods cannot be applied. The better approach is to address the question using the best evidence available. An incomplete answer to a critical question is better than no answer at all.

Granted, there are practical obstacles to shifting the focus of research toward bigger questions. Over the last forty years, academic institutions have been overhauled to encourage the sort of research favored within the public management approach. For example, PhD programs now provide a different sort of training than they did in the late 1970s, focused more intensely on middle-level questions and quantitative-statistical methods. It will take years to reorient PhD programs so that researchers have the theoretical and methodological equipment needed to address new questions. Then there is the problem of "perverse incentive structures."[14] Over the last forty years, academic personnel decisions—those in regard to hiring, compensation, tenure, and promotion—have become more closely tied to candidates' success in publishing in top-ranked journals. Many of these top-ranked journals give preference to research undertaken within the public management approach. Overall, the scholarly enterprise is more rigid and resistant to change than it was during the shift toward the public management approach in the late 1970s and early 1980s. For new scholars especially, exploring new approaches might be a career-limiting move.

There are, nonetheless, pathways toward reform. Senior scholars, less affected by perverse incentives, can make the case for pursuing new lines of research. Indeed, a growing number of senior scholars have done this in recent years, as I noted in the introduction. They are providing reassurance for junior scholars who want to justify deviations from the orthodoxy. The growth of scholarly institutions in Asia also provides an opportunity for scholars in that region to create a different set of incentive structures for new scholars. And new scholars themselves must find ways of pushing against orthodoxy about the appropriate boundaries of research. There is no way around this: the scholar's duty is to address questions that are important even when the pursuit of those questions is poorly rewarded.

Chapter 21

Teaching

Today, tens of thousands of students are enrolled in graduate programs in public administration or public affairs in the United States.[1] The mission of these programs is to educate leaders for public service. If we are considering a new approach toward the study of public administration, it is reasonable to ask whether our views about teaching public administration should change as well. Should the curriculum in public administration look different than it does today?

Yes, although the required adjustment is not radical. A graduate program that prepares leaders ought to have some component that shows how to think broadly about the overall aims of government, the factors and forces that influence judgments about priorities, the previous methods used to advance those priorities, and how priorities and methods have adapted in response to changing conditions. In other words, there ought to be some element of the curriculum that shows students how to think systematically about the challenges of crafting, executing, and adapting strategies for governing. This sort of education would encourage students to take a long view. They would look decades back to see how strategies have evolved and decades ahead to anticipate new challenges. And there would be a comparative aspect as well: students would learn how the leaders of other countries wrestle with comparable challenges.

Broadly speaking, graduate programs in public administration in the United States do not train students to think systematically about the big picture. A glance at the curricula of many well-regarded graduate programs reveals that they focus on the middle level of public service: on problems of policy design, management within public organizations, and the implementation and evaluation of programs.[2] When prospective managers and analysts are encouraged to take a wider view, to look upward and outward, it is often with the purpose of understanding their "authorizing environment"; that is, the constellation of actors in the immediate neighborhood of the agency or program that have a direct influence on its behavior.[3] This perspective is quite different from a broad and long view of the processes by which government as a whole evolves. For example, it is the difference between understanding the prerequisites for success for an agency embedded within the welfare state and understanding the welfare state itself—the reasons for its existence and its path of development. Some readers might be tempted to say that questions about the purpose and design of the welfare state are better left to political scientists. But the blueprints for the welfare state were drawn by practitioners and scholars in public administration, so it would be a little strange to say that their successors should not revisit them.[4] The same could be said about the blueprints for the modern regulatory state or the national security state, also drafted by scholars in public administration.

A few graduate programs in public administration encourage a broader view by requiring students to complete an overview course on "public administration and democracy" or "public administration and society."[5] These courses have limitations, however. Sometimes they simply push the "authorizing environment" perspective a little further, so that students can see how agency operations are affected by overall institutional and social context. These courses may refer to important recent trends such as globalization and technological change, but there is no systematic survey of all factors that shape strategies for governing. And the focus is exclusively on the United States.[6] The possibility that leaders of other countries wrestle with comparable problems and might have discovered alternative strategies for governing is usually overlooked.

How else could a curriculum in public administration be organized? For an alternative approach, look to leading graduate programs in international relations—many of which also say that they are in the business of preparing leaders for public service.[7] At the School of Advanced International Studies at Johns Hopkins University, students must complete a course called Theories of International Relations, which

> surveys a variety of broad theoretical approaches to analyzing the international political and economic situation [and] examines approaches to the study of power, ideology, state interests, peace and war, international law, and equilibrium; presents a critique of liberal, conservative and Marxist conceptions of international politics; and introduces grand theory, political and economic interpretations of systems structure and the values that shape perspectives in international politics.[8]

At the School of Foreign Service at Georgetown University, meanwhile, students complete a course in the theory and practice of international relations, through which they

> (a) gain deep knowledge of the dominant theories of international relations;
> (b) [learn how] to confidently assess the explanatory power of these theories in the study and practice of international politics;
> (c) engage in a sophisticated and effective way with the most pressing contemporary policy debates in international politics.[9]

And at Columbia University, graduate students in international relations complete a course called Conceptual Foundations of International Politics, which is

> designed to help students think theoretically and analytically about leading issues in international affairs by introducing them to social science methods and scholarship and by exposing them to the uses of such concepts in practice, through examination of contemporary problems and challenges in international affairs.[10]

The administrators of graduate programs in international relations, like their peers in public administration, wrestle with the problem of rationing time in a short professional degree. Still, space is found in the international relations curriculum for courses that take a broad and systematic view of the conditions confronting leaders. The curriculum recognizes that students must "recognize the underlying forces at work in the world . . . [and learn how] to navigate a changing landscape."[11] It is taken for granted that courses such as these are essential for professional success.[12] Further, the approach of international relations programs is cosmopolitan. The United States is treated as one state among many: *primus inter pares*, perhaps, but still wrestling with problems that are shared with other states.

Many people agree that globalization has blurred the line between domestic and foreign affairs; however, there is still this difference in professional training for public service in the realms of domestic and foreign policy. The better approach is one taken by graduate programs in international relations, which are conscious of the big picture, inclined toward the long view, and attentive to challenges of statecraft. The same sensibility ought to be cultivated within graduate programs of public administration. There, too, students should know how to recognize and navigate a changing landscape—that is, how to craft, implement, and adapt strategies for governing.

Chapter 22

Practice

My intention has been to develop a new way of thinking about public administration. The goal is not only to improve research and teaching but also, ultimately, to improve professional practice. We can do this in two ways.

Most directly, we can show leaders how to improve in crafting, executing, and adapting strategies for governing. As I noted in chapter 5, all leaders use some sort of strategy to guide their decision-making, but these strategies may be poorly reasoned simply because leaders are unaware that they are engaged in strategy-making. As a result, they make strategies unconsciously and haphazardly. Our purpose should be to show leaders how strategy-making can be done deliberately, through an explicit assessment of goals, contexts, and methods. In particular, we want leaders to think carefully about the challenge of executing strategy through the design and administration of state institutions. Decisions about strategy ought to be driven by an understanding of what institutions can or cannot do, as well as an understanding of the work involved in renovating existing institutions and building new ones. The connection between strategy and state architecture is critical, and it is a subject in which public administration scholars should have distinctive competence.

The need for leaders to think carefully about strategy varies over time. There are periods of calm when the prevailing strategy—the conventional wisdom about the ends and means of government—seems to work well and is given little thought. I might even say that in these periods, leaders give strategy too little thought: they become overconfident and think that they have discovered a permanent formula for governing. In these moments, scholars may also take the overall strategy as a given and focus instead on details of execution. Arguably that is what happened in the 1990s and early 2000s, in the heyday of neoliberalism and public management. But these periods of calm never last for more than a few years, and when they end, leaders are forced to revisit the basic questions of strategy. These are typically painful moments in national affairs. The pain is aggravated because leaders and scholars are caught flat-footed. They are out of practice in thinking about the fundamentals of strategy. Perhaps they have even forgotten the basic point that strategies are fragile, that they must inevitably be renovated, and that, in fact, they have been renovated successfully many times in the past. As John Dewey said in 1927, "the state must always be rediscovered." Forgetting all this, they may think darkly that the country has reached the end of the road and that the American state is on the cusp of failure.[1] The pain of adjustment would be assuaged if the capacity to think deliberately about strategy were maintained in good times as well as bad. This would help to break the cycle of hubris and despair that sometimes affects American politics.

A deliberate conversation about the challenges of strategy-making would also encourage leaders and citizens to think about what can be learned from other countries. We would break the bad habit of parochialism within American public administration and lay the groundwork for a cross-national conversation about designing strategies that are effective in promoting security, prosperity, and human rights.

There will be an urgent need for this sort of conversation in coming years. The twenty-first century is likely to be one in which the distribution of power within the state system shifts away from the West to countries like China and India. The great question will be how these vast and populous countries can be governed effectively. Chinese leaders believe that they have a formula that is robust even though it rejects the liberal democratic model. They are increasingly forthright in questioning the American way of governing.[2] Scholars of public administration must prepare for debate about the relative merits of democratic and non-democratic strategies for governing—just as they did in the 1930s and 1940s.

Even at lower levels of administration, there is value in understanding how strategies for governing are invented, executed, and adapted. Public servants who have no role in shaping the prevailing strategy are nonetheless obliged to work within it. Decisions at the meso- and micro-levels of public administration are constrained by choices at the macro-level.[3] There is a conventional wisdom about national priorities and the role of government that makes certain lower-level policies politically feasible and others infeasible.[4] In the 1990s, for example, the fashion was for market-friendly policies, and policies that required bureaucratic and regulatory expansion were out of favor. Thirty years earlier, the fashion went the other way. Policy analysts and managers who want to understand which administrative practices will be favored at any particular moment in history must know which way the winds are blowing. To make the case for reforms at lower levels of government, they must understand the higher-level strategy and how their own reform plans cohere with it.

The same kind of knowledge is required when thinking about the transfer of practices from one country to another. A practice that works in one country may be infeasible in another if the leaders in those countries have different ideas about overall strategy. As noted in the introduction, many Asian scholars have criticized the importation of policies from the United States and other market-oriented Western democracies. The probability that Western practices will be adopted and properly implemented is said to be "mediated by . . . the strategies of the governing elites" in Asian countries.[5] Again, a conversation about the big picture cannot be avoided.

As we have seen, this is not a new idea. This is what Woodrow Wilson had in mind when he wrote in his famous essay of 1887 that the state is "the conscience of administration."[6] Judgments about administrative technique cannot be separated from judgments about the role and design of the state. Louis Brownlow, another pioneer of American public administration, served Woodrow Wilson as one of the presidentially appointed managers of the

District of Columbia from 1915 to 1920. "He taught me many things about administration," Brownlow recalled. "But he was first of all and always the statesman, and he based his statesmanship on politics, high politics, the grand politics of a leader of men."[7] We must recover that wider view about the aims of public administration.

Conclusion

Grand Challenges

The National Academy of Public Administration is an American nonprofit organization that was established with a charter from the U.S. Congress in 1967. Its purpose is to help government leaders solve critical management problems.[1] In November 2018, the academy announced a new project. It made a public call for comments about the "grand challenges of public administration." Specifically, it sought advice on two questions, capitalizing for emphasis: "WHAT government must do over the next decade and HOW it should do it."[2]

This was an unusual venture for the academy, which typically gives advice to executives within federal departments and agencies, examining administrative practices and making recommendations for improvement. With this project, the academy pitched its concerns more broadly. It asked about national priorities, the main lines of government policy, and implications for the organization of government. In other words, the academy wondered what the strategy for governing the United States should be in the coming decade.

The academy posed these questions in 2018 because there was confusion about what the strategy ought to be. There had been a rough consensus on strategy in the decade or so before the financial crisis of 2007–2008. America's governing class, and most of its citizens, were generally skeptical about "big government" and supportive of free trade and internationalism. As I observed in chapter 5, this governance strategy had been launched by Republican President Ronald Reagan in the 1980s and then refined and ratified by Democratic President Bill Clinton in the 1990s.[3] In the United Kingdom, a comparable strategy was introduced by Conservative Prime Minister Margaret Thatcher in the 1980s and ratified by Labour Prime Minister Tony Blair in the 1990s.

The Reagan-Clinton strategy began to wobble in the early 2000s and was seriously destabilized by the financial crisis and its aftermath. The world changed, and, as a result, the strategy no longer seemed as effective in achieving the fundamentals: security, internal order and comity, prosperity and justice. A surge in terrorism made people uneasy about open borders and briefly more tolerant of military adventurism. Growing inequality and insecurity caused second thoughts about economic laissez-fairism. The rise of China, and its failure to pursue economic and political liberalization, led to doubts about free trade and accommodative diplomacy. Technological innovations disturbed the economy, society, and politics.

Eventually the gap between strategy and reality became too wide, and agreement about its virtues broke down entirely. Between 1996 and 2003, the heyday of the Reagan-Clinton strategy, a solid majority of Americans said they were satisfied with the way things were going for the country, according to the Gallup Poll. By contrast, only a quarter expressed satisfaction in the decade after 2007.[4] The 2016 presidential election exposed the frailty of the Reagan-Clinton formula and deep divisions about what ought to replace it. Fifty-eight million people voted in the Democratic and Republican primaries in 2016. Only twenty-seven percent voted for Hillary Clinton, who was closely tied to the old formula. Twenty-two percent voted for Bernie Sanders, a self-declared socialist. Twenty-four percent voted for Donald Trump, an ethno-nationalist who favored less government intervention in some aspects of social and economic policy and more intervention in other aspects. Confusion and polarization over strategy persisted after the 2016 election.

This was not the first time that the United States found itself in such a muddle.[5] The country went through a comparable process of strategic collapse and reinvention in 1930s and 1940s. This led to a post-war order that put more emphasis on economic planning and activist social policy, among other things. There was another readjustment in the 1970s, as the post-war formula broke down: this eventually led to the Reagan-Clinton strategy. There were earlier readjustments as well. In general, these shifts in strategy do not happen quickly. Two decades passed between the crash of 1929 and the emergence of a new consensus about governance strategy in the late 1940s and early 1950s.[6] Similarly, two decades passed between the confusion of the early 1970s and Clinton's affirmation of the new strategy in the mid-1990s. If history is a guide, therefore, we should not be surprised by the persistence of political confusion only a decade after the financial crisis of 2007–2008.

This history also suggests that the timeframe proposed by NAPA in its call for comments was too short. NAPA asked what problems would face American government over the next decade—but it might take another decade just to define and consolidate a new strategy for governing. As I argued in chapter 12, we ought to look further into the future, thinking about challenges that will confront American government over the next thirty to fifty years. In fact, several government agencies use longer timeframes in their long-term planning.[7]

However, the main difficulty with NAPA's project was not the timeframe. NAPA specifically invited academics, students, and practitioners in the field of public administration to address its two broad questions. And it was certainly possible for people in the field to compose an answer. However, these questions were not routinely addressed within the field of public administration in 2018. It was not as though people could reprise arguments already at hand about the WHAT and HOW of government. Leading journals in public administration did not publish many articles on these broad questions. Conferences were not regularly organized around them, and graduate programs generally did not teach students how to think systematically about them. In short, addressing grand challenges was not one of the field's distinctive competencies.

As I said earlier in the introduction, this deficiency did not come about by accident. It was the result of decisions taken deliberately by leaders within the field over the last forty years. The scholars and practitioners who invented the field a century ago certainly talked and wrote about grand challenges, with a determination to think systematically about questions of WHAT and HOW. Then the field changed direction. After the 1970s, we prized scholarship on meso-level rather than macro-level questions. Attention shifted because the legitimacy problems of Western governments appeared to be rooted in failures at the meso-level, and because it seemed easier to conduct rigorous research at that level.

Still, it was shortsighted to run down our skills in addressing macro-level questions, because it was inevitable that we would find ourselves in a moment like this. History shows us that governance strategies are fragile and bound to break down eventually (see chapter 9). In moments of strategic collapse, the question of whether Agency X is operating with optimal efficiency is not of foremost importance. Rather, we are concerned with the architecture of government as a whole and whether it is designed to achieve national priorities, given the prevailing conditions. As Walter Lippmann said a century ago, the aim is to adjust government to the facts of the modern world.[8]

The field of public administration has been caught out at a critical moment. The problems that will confront the American state in the mid-twenty-first century are no less substantial than those of Lippman's time. Climatic disruption, shifts in the global power balance, demographic changes, technological revolutions, fiscal pressures, infrastructural shortfalls—all of these trends could jeopardize security, order, and citizens' well-being if government does not anticipate the dangers and organize itself properly in response. And we know from experience that it takes years to build agreement on strategy and reconstruct institutions so that they give expression to it. Choices made in the next few years will shape the contours of American public administration for decades to come.

The pioneers of American public administration were aware that there was a third big question, in addition to the Academy's WHAT and HOW: whether states that adhered to liberal democratic principles were capable of rising to new challenges at all. There was considerable doubt about the resilience of liberal democracies in the early decades of the twentieth century. Many people thought that authoritarian systems—fascism in Germany and Italy, communism in the Soviet Union—had the edge in dealing with problems of the modern age. The assignment for American specialists in public administration was to prove the skeptics wrong: that states could achieve security, order, and prosperity while also preserving democracy and fundamental rights.

We face the same assignment today. The reputation of liberal democracy has been battered over the past decade. As a result, some countries have turned toward populist authoritarianism. In 2014, for example, Hungarian president Viktor Orbán renounced "liberal methods and principles of organizing a society," declaring that liberal systems could not survive in the "great world-race" among nations.[9] Other leaders have also embraced Orbán's model of "illiberal democracy."[10] And there are states that reject both liberalism and democracy. China—which is likely to have the world's largest economy within the next two decades—is consolidating a system of one-party authoritarianism. Defenders of the Chinese system argue that it avoids the "deep-seated problems of the political model developed in the West."[11] Western scholars, like their predecessors in the 1930s, must show that these problems are transient, and not intrinsic to liberal democracy; that current discontent is just a side effect of strategic exhaustion; and that liberal democracies can adapt to new conditions. Of course, this requires that scholars put their ideological cards on the table. We must be clear that our aim is not just "good governance," but good liberal-democratic governance.

More candor about first principles is not the only adjustment necessary within public administration. The field must rebuild the capacity to address grand challenges. We can begin by acknowledging the importance of macro-level questions and rewarding young scholars who choose to explore them. Conference organizers, journal editors, and teachers should create space for conversation about these questions. We will need patience as we develop the conceptual toolkit and the shared vocabulary that is essential to constructive conversation. We must explore history and the experience of other states to understand the diverse ways in which macro-level questions have been answered. And we must accept the need for informed speculation as well as well-grounded empirical research. There is no statistical analysis that will resolve the question of how leaders should anticipate climatic disruption, workplace automation, or the emergence of new superpowers. In the end, we must use our imagination as we craft strategies for governing that are effective, durable, and true to our ideals.

A Glossary of States

Academics constantly discover and label new types of states. Sometimes their labels relate to features or circumstances (for example, fragile states or frontier states), and sometimes they relate to the priorities and strategies of leaders (for example, developmental states or welfare states). The practice of labeling states is problematic, however, because no single adjective adequately describes all of the important conditions that influence strategy or all of the critical aspects of the strategy itself. In other words, the practice is far too reductive. Still, it is useful to note the many types of states identified over the last century. It is a reminder that leaders respond in many ways to diverse circumstances and also that states change form constantly. This glossary defines some of the most important state-types that have been identified over the last century.

Administrative state. This is a state that has acquired an extensive bureaucracy with responsibilities for regulating economic and social affairs. Introduced in the early 1940s, this term is usually used in discussions about the problems of accountability that arise as a consequence of delegating rulemaking and adjudicative power to administrative agencies.[1] A related concept, introduced by James Burnham in 1941, is the *managerial state*. Burnham argued that all major political systems were preoccupied with economic planning and that, as a result, "the institutions of the state [are] . . . the 'property' of the managers."[2] The advent of the administrative state was sometimes regarded as a necessary response to the concentration of economic power within the private sector. A similar idea was conveyed in J. K. Galbraith's description of the *new industrial state* in 1967: one in which government agencies are actively involved in economic planning and work closely with large corporations, and in which power lies in the hands of the specialists who constitute society's "technostructure."[3]

City-state. A city-state has a relatively small territory and a population that is concentrated in a single urban area. Modern examples are Singapore, Monaco, and Qatar.[4] The contrast is sometimes made to *territorial states*, which are more expansive and have many urban centers as well as a large population living outside urban areas.[5] City-states may have been more consequential before the modern era. Italy was organized as a network of rival city-states until the sixteenth century; this is the world described by Machiavelli in *The Prince*. The city-state was also the building block of political order in Ancient Greece.[6]

Civilian state. This term was introduced by Harold Lasswell in 1941 as a contrast to the *garrison state* (see below). It was revived by James Sheehan in 2007 to describe the states of contemporary Europe. These are states that have "retained the capacity to make war with one another but lost all interest in doing so." Sheehan argued that the military role of these states was eclipsed by their obligations to promote economic growth, social welfare, and personal development. These are states "organized for peace, not war."[7]

Civilization-state or civilizational state. This term was introduced in the 1990s with particular reference to India and China. The civilization state is one that has an unusually large population and territory, often with substantial linguistic, cultural, or religious diversity, but is still bound together at a fundamental level by shared values, history, and traditions. Such a state is thought to have a special duty to preserve the civilization contained within it.[8]

Deep state. This term was coined by Turkish Prime Minister Bülent Ecevit in 1974 to describe a hidden network of officials within security and intelligence agencies and the judiciary, that exercises power in collaboration with leaders of organized crime without regard to the law.[9] This hidden network puts "extreme emphasis on state security."[10] Recently, the concept has been adapted to the American context. Mike Lofgren has defined the American deep state as "a hybrid association of key elements of government and parts of top-level finance and industry that is effectively able to govern the United States with only limited reference to the consent of the governed as normally expressed through elections."[11]

Developmental state. This term was introduced in the early 1970s to describe poor states in which government takes an active role in guiding economic development, with the goal of catching up to industrialized nations.[12] Such a state may assume responsibility for "major allocative and production decisions . . . [and] the social and cultural transformations" that are necessary for industrialization. These states may discourage popular mobilization, while legitimating state action by "cloaking it in the mystique of technology."[13] In 1982 Chalmers Johnson described Japan as a developmental state, arguing that this form had enabled the extraordinary economic growth of the preceding three decades. The Japanese developmental state was distinguished by a powerful and prestigious national bureaucracy, exemplified by the Ministry of International Trade and Industry (MITI), which defined national economic goals and actively coordinated public and private behavior to achieve those goals.[14] Taiwan and South Korea have also been described as developmental states.

Empire. This is a system of governance "in which one state controls the effective political sovereignty of another political society."[15] The state exercising control is sometimes referred to by scholars as the metropole, while dependent societies constitute the periphery. Imperial states often claim a civilizing function: they "export their characteristic institutions to the periphery, thereby building a bridge between the two and creating a common culture that ensures that metropolitan institutions and ideas always have the upper hand."[16] Limited powers of self-government may be granted to peripheral societies, perhaps with authority limited to a settler population. The most prominent empire in the late nineteenth century was Britain's, although other major European powers also maintained empires until World War I. The United States briefly experimented with the imperial model when it acquired territories after the Spanish-American War.[17] The idea of empire has been applied in a different sense by Hardt and Negri: "The decline in sovereignty in nation-states . . . does not mean that sovereignty as such has declined. . . . Sovereignty has taken a new form, composed of a series of national and supranational organisms united under a single logic of rule. This new global form of sovereignty is what we call Empire."[18]

Fiscal-military state. This term was coined in the late 1980s to describe the British state of the eighteenth century, and it was subsequently applied to other European states of that era. Such a state is competent in collecting taxes and managing expenditures and debts, primarily because these tasks are critical to maintaining a large military force and prosecuting wars with other states.[19]

Fragile states, failed states, and areas of limited statehood. The idea of a fragile state was introduced in the 1960s to describe the predicament of countries, notably in Africa, that were struggling to establish themselves after achieving independence from imperial powers. The concept of the failed state, one that is unable to perform the most basic functions such as maintaining order within its territory, was introduced in the early 1990s and applied to new states established after the collapse of the Soviet Union. Such states are often burdened with poverty, ethnic divisions, and the lack of a "tradition of statehood or practice in self-government." They are wracked by violence and political instability and may be "simply unable to function as independent entities."[20] The concept of "areas of limited statehood" was introduced around 2009 to describe "those parts of a country in which central authorities . . . lack the ability to implement and enforce rules and decisions."[21]

Frontier state. This is a state preoccupied with extending rule over a vast internal hinterland, often displacing indigenous populations. In this kind of state, the frontier marks the boundary between the settled core and the unsettled edges.[22] Examples include the United States, Russia, Brazil, and Canada. Although usage of this term is new, the underlying idea is not. Frederick Jackson Turner argued that American history until 1890 was "in a large degree the history of the colonization of the Great West.... The peculiarity of American institutions is the fact that they have been compelled to adapt themselves to the changes of an expanding people—to the changes involved in crossing a continent, in winning a wilderness, and in developing at each area of this progress out of the primitive economic and political conditions of the frontier into the complexity of city life."[23]

Garrison state, warfare state, and national security state. In 1941, Harold Lasswell predicted the rise of *garrison states* led by military personnel skilled in "modern civilian management." This state would have an expanded role in coordinating economic activity to support military strength; meanwhile, democratic institutions would weaken, political competition and dissent would be actively discouraged, and propaganda would become important for maintaining support of the regime.[24] The notion of the *warfare state* was introduced in 1962 to describe the United States, which was said to be increasingly dominated by the armed services and preoccupied with national security concerns.[25] The same notion was captured by the idea of the *national security state*, introduced later in the 1960s.[26] This sort of state was distinguished by a tight connection between the military establishment and private industry; in 1961, President Eisenhower called this the military-industrial complex.[27]

Hollow state. This term was introduced in the 1990s, with particular reference to the United States. It describes a state in which central government has been "hollowed out" because of the devolution of administrative responsibilities to lower levels of government, contractors, and nonprofit agencies. This state is said to suffer from serious problems of control, coordination, and accountability for the provision of public services.[28]

Market state. This term was introduced around 2000 to describe a state in which overall economic management is left in the hands of international capital markets and multinational business networks rather than governments; the state is regarded as a "minimal redistributor," and its main aim is to promote economic opportunity. Emphasis is put on incentives and penalties to achieve desired outcomes rather than on compulsion by law, and the influence of traditional democratic institutions is reduced.[29]

Multinational state. This term was introduced in the late 1930s to describe a state in which a significant proportion of citizens "speak distinct languages and cherish diverse historical and cultural memories." This kind of state was presumed to suffer increased risks of instability because of its linguistic and cultural diversity.[30] (See *nation-state* below.)

Nation-state. This term was first used in the late nineteenth century to describe a state with a population that "is of one nativity, and that shares the other similarities of custom and culture which usually accompany unity of blood ... so that the state is bound together, not alone by political authority, but also by sharing, if not literally in the national blood, yet in the national patriotism, ideals, customs, economic and cultural life-current."[31] Earlier, John Stuart Mill had argued that "free institutions are next to impossible in a country made up of different nationalities. Among a people without fellow-feeling, especially if they read and speak different languages, the united public opinion, necessary to the working of representative government, cannot exist."[32] More recently, Adrian Hastings has defined a nation-state as one in which people are seen "as a horizontally bonded society to whom the state in a sense belongs."[33]

Neoliberal state. This term was introduced in the mid-1980s to describe a state that limits its role in economic affairs and restricts services and benefits associated with the welfare state. In this state, barriers to international trade and finance are lowered. Although the role of the state is limited, it is not weak: it retains the capacity to act decisively, protect property rights, maintain sound currency and fiscal discipline, provide an infrastructure essential to trade, limit the capacity of workers to mobilize, and prevent disruption through protest.[34] A related concept is that of the *competition state*, introduced by Philip Cerny in 1990.[35]

Network state. In 1989 Daniel Okimoto referred to Japan as a *network state*, able to exercise power not because of its formal organization or "structural characteristics" but because of its dense network of informal ties with the private sector.[36] In 1996, Manuel Castells also described the advent of a "new form of state, the network state," which he described as a "functional response" to the inability of the "obsolete nation-state" to respond effectively to the "growing strength of global networks of capital, information, communication, and crime."[37] Castells offered the European Union as "the most advanced example" of a network state. Such states are distinguished by "the sharing of a unified economy" and "the sharing of authority ... along a network" but also by the weakening of traditional democratic institutions, which contributes to a crisis of legitimacy.[38]

Night-watchman state or laissez-faire state. These terms were introduced in the late nineteenth century to describe a state whose "sole function ... is to protect the personal freedom and property of the individual"[39] or whose "sole business is to provide conditions whereby those who live within its jurisdiction may lead an existence secure against violence and illegal interference, and by which it will be made possible for them, unhindered except by such legal restrictions as are necessary to community life, to pursue their own interests with perfect freedom."[40] This conception of the state was associated with the Manchester school of economic liberalism.

Ordoliberal state. This term was introduced in the mid-1940s to describe the German conception of a strong state that plays an active role in maintaining a well-functioning market economy. Such a state assures a sound currency while rigorously enforcing anti-monopoly rules and prudent fiscal policies. The government's role in economic management is strictly governed by principles embedded in statute or constitutional law. As a result, government can assure a market economy that does not degenerate into chaos, while also minimizing the risk that governmental power itself will be abused.[41] This conception of the state emerged as a reaction to the economic and political instability of the Weimar period. It was regarded as a mode of liberal governance that would avoid the risk of collapse into authoritarian rule.

Party-state or one-party state. This is a state in which there is no clear boundary between the administrative apparatus of government and the ruling party. By implication, there are no opposition parties that can actually attain control of government, since this would imply a complete reconstruction of the administrative apparatus. For example, the rule of the Popular Movement for the Liberation of Angola (MPLA) has been described as "a party-state structure of domination in which conventional boundaries between party, state and public administration are virtually meaningless."[42] Similarly, China has been described as a system in which the Communist Party "controls the entire public sector. . . . [It] staffs government ministries and agencies through an elaborate and opaque appointments system [and] instructs them on policy through behind-the-scenes committees."[43] China has also been described as a Leninist party-state, because party control over government, the military, and society is so deeply institutionalized.[44]

Petro-state. This term was introduced in the mid-1970s to describe a state that derives a substantial amount of revenue from the exploitation of oil reserves. Easy access to oil revenues may undermine incentives for leaders to develop effective methods of collecting taxes and managing expenditures carefully. At the same time, lavish revenues may increase public demand for state services, competition for control of the state, and the risk of corruption within the state. Such states also wrestle with the "Dutch disease"—that is, the declining competitiveness of other sectors caused by oil exports skewing currency exchange rates.[45]

Police state or secret police state. The notion of the *police state* was popularized in the late 1940s to describe regimes like those in the Soviet Union and fascist Europe. It is a state in which civil liberties are severely restricted and internal security services maintain order through intensive surveillance and repression of dissent. A police state, R. A. Hasson suggested in 1966, is one in which there is "extreme intolerance of any form of political opposition and delegation of far-reaching and drastic powers to the police."[46]

Positive state. This term was first used around 1900 to describe a state that repudiates the laissez-faire doctrine that government functions should be restricted so far as possible. Instead, this state uses its power to promote the public welfare; for example, through the regulation of trust, workplace conditions, and food safety. In the United States, the concept was advocated by progressive reformers such as Herbert Croly.[47]

Predatory state. This term was introduced in the early 1970s to describe states in which officeholders are not constrained by law and enrich themselves by preying upon the ruled. In such a state, "brigandage is the predominant form of power."[48] Larry Diamond observes, "The purpose of government [in a predatory state] is not to generate public goods, such as roads, schools, clinics, and sewer systems. Instead, it is to produce private goods for officials, their families, and their cronies."[49]

Protectorates and protected states. These states retain internal autonomy, but their foreign policy is determined by another state in exchange for the promise of protection by that state.

Regulatory state. This term, introduced around 1950, was initially used to describe states that had abandoned the policy of laissez-faire in the late nineteenth century. These states had begun to use law more actively to limit market abuses, but had not yet moved to the stage of directly producing extensive public services, as welfare states do.[50] But the term has also been used to describe the American state of the late twentieth century, because of the expansion of regulatory functions in the postwar era.[51] The term became popular in Europe after 1990 as well, to describe a state that relied principally on rulemaking as an instrument for economic management rather than on more intrusive techniques, such as public ownership, centralized planning, or extensive public spending.[52]

Rogue state. This term was introduced in the 1990s to describe states that refuse to respect international law or to negotiate interstate conflicts in good faith, and whose behavior threatens the security of other states. In the 1990s, policymakers in the United States described North Korea, Iraq, and Libya as rogue states.[53] After 2003, the United States itself was sometimes condemned as a rogue state because of its alleged indifference to international law as it invaded Iraq.[54]

States of emergency, states of exception, and states of siege. These terms do not describe a kind of state; rather, they describe conditions under which normal routines of government are suspended so that the executive can deal with an extraordinary threat to the state or society. A state of emergency usually involves suspending laws that protect civil liberties and also requirements for legislative authorization of executive actions.[55] Some states explicitly establish procedures for granting emergency powers to the executive. Others do it implicitly, as the United States arguably did after the terror attacks of September 11, 2001. The same effect may be accomplished by proclaiming a *state of martial law*. Arend Lijphart suggested that states that do not revert to normal routines can be described as *emergency regimes*.[56] Similarly, David Unger has recently described the United States as a *permanent emergency state*: a "complex of national security institutions, reflexes, and beliefs . . . [dedicated to] permanent crisis management."[57]

Submerged state.   This phrase was coined by Suzanne Mettler in 2001 to describe the condition of the contemporary American state. Such a state pursues its objectives by "by providing incentives, subsidies, or payments to private organizations or households to encourage or reimburse them for conducting activities deemed to serve a public purpose." These programs "remain largely invisible to ordinary Americans. . . . Their hallmark is the way they obscure government's role." Thus it is possible to sustain a political discourse that "espouses the virtues of small government" while the role of government expands: "Even when people stare directly at these policies, many perceive only a freely functioning market system at work."[58] Brian Balogh has argued that this is actually a longstanding feature of the American state. Even in the nineteenth century, Americans preferred a government that was active but whose actions were designed to minimize the visibility of the state.[59]

Welfare state.   This term was coined by the British theologian William Temple in 1928 but entered into wider usage around 1939–1940 to describe a state that has a "positive mission of controlling and directing economic forces so as to promote social well-being." Such as state manages the economy to assure full employment; it also seeks to improve access to education, healthcare, and housing, and insure against risks of unemployment, disability, or indigence.[60] Stephen Spencer contrasted the welfare state with a *power-state* like that of Germany before World War I, which was interested in maximized state power rather than the wellbeing of subjects. The intellectual foundation for the post-World War II welfare state was established in Britain by the Beveridge Report of 1942 and in the United States by contemporaneous reports of the National Resources Planning Board.[61] In early years, the welfare state was also called the *social welfare state*, the *positive welfare state*, or the *social services state*.

Westphalian state.   This scholarly term was introduced in the 1960s to describe a form of governance that emerged three centuries earlier.[62] The Peace of Westphalia was established by a set of treaties signed in

1648 that concluded the Thirty Years' War and marked the de facto end of the Holy Roman Empire. It is regarded as the event that established the basic features of the modern state system, in which states are acknowledged to have "the entire right of sovereignty over their territory, together with the power of making war, concluding peace, and forming alliances."[63] In fact, though, the treaties still recognized important limitations of the autonomy of states.[64] In the 1990s, the related concept of Westphalian sovereignty was introduced, usually for the purpose of explaining how this was being undermined by globalization. The end result was said to be the *post-Westphalian state*, which shares its power with subnational and transnational political authorities.[65]

Further Reading

My thinking on this subject has evolved over several years. The following pieces may be consulted for elaboration of the argument in the introduction:

Milward, H. Brinton, Laura Jensen, Alasdair Roberts, Mauricio I. Dussauge-Laguna, Veronica Junjan, René Torenvlied, Arjen Boin, H. K. Colebatch, Donald Kettl, and Robert F. Durant. "Is Public Management Neglecting the State?" *Governance* 29, no. 3 (2016): 1–26.

Roberts, Alasdair. "The Aims of Public Administration: Reviving the Classical View." *Perspectives on Public Management and Governance* 1, no. 1 (2018): 1–13.

———. "Bridging Levels of Public Administration: How Macro Shapes Meso and Micro." Working paper, March 2019. https://papers.ssrn.com/sol3/papers.cfm?abstract_id=3291763.

———. *Four Crises of American Democracy: Representation, Mastery, Discipline, Anticipation*. New York: Oxford University Press, 2017. Chapter 6.

———. *Large Forces: What's Missing in Public Administration*. North Charleston, SC: CreateSpace, 2013.

———. "The Path Not Taken: Leonard White and the Macrodynamics of Administrative Development." *Public Administration Review* 69, no. 4 (2009): 764–775.

———. "Strategies for Governing: An Approach to Public Management Research for West and East." *Korean Journal of Policy Studies* 33, no. 1 (2018): 33–56.

———. "What's Wrong with the Intellectual History of Public Administration?" *Public Voices* 11, no. 2 (2010): 10–15.

And here is a brief, illustrative list of books that have proved useful in developing my ideas about strategies for governing:

Barraclough, Geoffrey. *An Introduction to Contemporary History*. Harmondsworth, UK: Penguin, 1967.
Though now dated, this book is an impressive attempt to think broadly about the forces that shape societies and their governments.
Benner, Erica. *Be Like the Fox: Machiavelli in His World*. New York, W. W. Norton, 2017.
An excellent overview of Machiavelli's life and worldview.
Cannadine, David. *The Undivided Past: History beyond Our Differences*. London: Penguin, 2014.
A survey of major social cleavages (although it neglects conflict between urban and rural populations and between metropoles and peripheries).
Crawford, James. *The Creation of States in International Law*. New York: Oxford University Press, 2006.
A discussion of the conditions for recognizing states under international law.
Donnelly, Jack. *Universal Human Rights in Theory and Practice*. 3rd ed. Ithaca, NY: Cornell University Press, 2013.
An examination of the postwar movement to define and protect human rights.
Finer, S. E. *The History of Government from the Earliest Times*. 3 vols. Oxford: Oxford University Press, 1997.
A comprehensive canvas of the evolution of governmental institutions.
Foucault, Michel. *Security, Territory, Population: Lectures at the Collège de France, 1977–78*. Basingstoke, UK: Palgrave Macmillan, 2007.
A discussion on the emergence of modern states and the development of *raison d'etat* (see chapter 4).
Freedman, Lawrence. *Strategy: A History*. New York: Oxford University Press, 2013.
A comprehensive history of strategic thinking.
Fukuyama, Francis. *Political Order and Political Decay*. New York: Farrar, Straus & Giroux, 2014.
Concerns about the failure of the American state to adapt to new challenges (expressed in the latter part of the book).
Hood, Christopher. *The Art of the State*. New York: Clarendon, 1998.
Hood, Christopher, and Ruth Dixon. *A Government That Worked Better and Cost Less?* Oxford: Oxford University Press, 2015.
An examination of the "public management revolution" of the late twentieth century and its effects in the United Kingdom.
Kennedy, Paul M. *The Rise and Fall of the Great Powers: Economic Change and Military Conflict from 1500 to 2000*. New York: Vintage, 1987.

An application of the concept of grand strategy to the domain of international relations.

Kulman, Linda. *Teaching Common Sense: The Grand Strategy Program at Yale University*. New Haven, CT: Prospecta, 2016.

A description of how the concept of grand strategy is applied in graduate courses.

Mann, Michael. *The Sources of Social Power*. Vol. 3, *Global Empires and Revolution, 1890–1945*. New York: Cambridge University Press, 2012.

An examination of the techniques used by modern states to extend their influence.

McNeill, John Robert, and Peter Engelke. *The Great Acceleration: An Environmental History of the Anthropocene since 1945*. Cambridge, MA: Belknap, 2014.

An updated version of the long-range analysis attempted by Barraclough above.

Schuck, Peter H. *Why Government Fails So Often*. Princeton, NJ: Princeton University Press, 2014.

A sober assessment of weaknesses in the design and implementation of federal programs in the United States in the late twentieth and early twenty-first centuries.

Scott, James C. *Against the Grain: A Deep History of the Earliest States*. New Haven: Yale University Press, 2017.

Scott, James C. *Seeing Like a State*. New Haven, CT: Yale University Press, 1998.

An exploration of the motivations of leaders and the limits of state competence.

Sisk, Timothy D. *Statebuilding: Consolidating Peace after Civil War*. Cambridge: Polity, 2013.

A discussion of the travails of fragile states in the modern era.

Skinner, Quentin. *Machiavelli: A Very Short Introduction*. Oxford: Oxford University Press.

A good introduction to an early realist.

Tilly, Charles. *Big Structures, Large Processes, Huge Comparisons*. New York: Russell Sage Foundation, 1984.

A case for raising the level of analysis.

Vile, M.J.C. *Constitutionalism and the Separation of Powers*. 2nd ed. Indianapolis: Liberty Fund, 1998.

A description of how Western states have attempted to regulate the exercise of state power.

Watson, Adam. *The Evolution of International Society: A Comparative Historical Analysis*. London: Routledge, 2009.

An examination of the evolution of international order.

Notes

Introduction

1. Woodrow Wilson, "The Study of Administration," *Political Science Quarterly* 2, no. 2 (1887): 197–222, 201.
2. Niccolò Machiavelli, *The Essential Writings of Machiavelli* (New York: Modern Library, 2007), 23–24, 72, 94, 114, 149, 215, 253.
3. Luther H. Gulick, "Politics, Administration, and the 'New Deal,'" *Annals of the American Academy of Political and Social Science* 169 (1933): 55–66, 63.
4. Walter Lippmann, *Drift and Mastery* (New York: Mitchell Kennerley, 1914), 116.
5. William S. Neal, "Roosevelt Silent on Dictator Bill Rebuff," *Illinois State Journal*, April 9, 1938, 1.
6. Charles E. Merriam, "The Ends of Government," *American Political Science Review* 38, no. 1 (1944): 21–40, 21.
7. Walter Lippmann, *A Preface to Politics* (New York: Mitchell Kennerley, 1913), 18.
8. Lynton K. Caldwell, "The Relevance of Administrative History," *International Review of Administrative Sciences* 21, no. 3 (1955): 453–466, 461.
9. John M. Gaus, *Reflections on Public Administration* (University: University of Alabama Press, 1947), 8–9.

10. Charles E. Merriam, *Systematic Politics* (Chicago: University of Chicago Press, 1945), 37.

11. Leonard D. White, *Introduction to the Study of Public Administration*, 2nd ed. (New York: Macmillan, 1939), 34.

12. George A. Boyne, "The Intellectual Crisis in British Public Administration: Is Public Management the Problem or the Solution?," *Public Administration* 74, no. 4 (1996): 679–694, 679–680; Laurence E. Lynn Jr., "The Myth of the Bureaucratic Paradigm: What Traditional Public Administration Really Stood For," *Public Administration Review* 61, no. 2 (2001): 144–160, 144; Owen E. Hughes, *Public Management and Administration*, 3rd ed. (New York: Palgrave Macmillan, 2003), 45; John M. Bryson, Barbara C. Crosby, and Laura Bloomberg, "Public Value Governance: Moving Beyond Traditional Public Administration and the New Public Management," *Public Administration Review* 74, no. 4 (2014): 445–456, 445.

13. Jan-Erik Lane, "Will Public Management Drive out Public Administration?," *Asian Journal of Public Administration* 16, no. 2 (1994): 139–151, 139.

14. Early statements about the aims of the enterprise are provided by Laurence E. Lynn Jr., "Public Management: What Do We Know? What Should We Know? And How Will We Know It?," *Journal of Policy Analysis and Management* 7, no. 1 (1987): 178–187, 179–182; Barry Bozeman, *Public Management: The State of the Art* (San Francisco: Jossey-Bass, 1993), 362; Laurence E. Lynn Jr., "Public Management Research: The Triumph of Art over Science," *Journal of Policy Analysis and Management* 13, no. 2 (1994): 231–259, 231–233; Robert D. Behn, "The Big Questions of Public Management," *Public Administration Review* 55, no. 4 (1995): 313–324; Donald F. Kettl and H. Brinton Milward, *The State of Public Management* (Baltimore: Johns Hopkins University Press, 1996), 52–53; Jeffrey L. Brudney, Laurence J. O'Toole, and Hal G. Rainey, *Advancing Public Management* (Washington, DC: Georgetown University Press, 2000), 1–6; and Robert Agranoff and Michael McGuire, "Big Questions in Public Network Management Research," *Journal of Public Administration Research and Theory* 11, no. 3 (2001): 295–326. A summary of topics explored within the public management literature is provided by Stephen P. Osborne, "Public Management Research over the Decades: What Are We Writing About?," *Public Management Review* 19, no. 2 (2017): 109–113, 110.

15. H. George Frederickson et al., *The Public Administration Theory Primer*, 2nd ed. (Boulder, CO: Westview, 2012), 100. Similarly, Carolyn Hill and Laurence Lynn Jr. define public management as "the process of ensuring that the allocation and use of resources available to government are directed toward the achievement of lawful public policy goals": Carolyn J. Hill and Laurence E. Lynn Jr., *Public Management: Thinking and Acting in Three Dimensions*, 2nd ed. (Los Angeles: Sage, 2016), 5. In 2013, Kenneth Meier and Laurence O'Toole observed that the "growing field of public management has focused on the question of when and under what conditions management affects organizational performance." They identified two main questions: "Are public programs effective? And what is the role of public management in this regard?" Kenneth J. Meier and Laurence J. O'Toole, "Subjective Organizational Performance and Measurement Error: Common Source Bias and Spurious Relationships," *Journal of Public Administration Research and Theory* 23, no. 2 (2013): 429–456, 429–430.

16. Tony Bovaird and Elke Loeffler, *Public Management and Governance*, 3rd ed. (London: Routledge, 2016), 5.

17. David Osborne, "Reinventing Government," *Public Productivity and Management Review* 16, no. 4 (1993): 349–356, 350; Albert Gore, *Creating a Government That Works Better and Costs Less* (New York: Times, 1993).

18. Hughes, *Public Management and Administration*, 51. See also Laurence E. Lynn Jr., *Public Management: Old and New* (New York: Routledge, 2006), 104, and Christopher Pollitt and Geert Bouckaert, *Public Management Reform: A Comparative Analysis* (New York: Oxford University Press, 2011), 6.

19. In the United States, the advent of the "public management" orientation was also connected with the rise of graduate schools that specialized in public policy rather than public administration. These schools were dominated by economists and had a technocratic orientation, concerned primarily with the design and implementation of solutions to policy problems. These schools displaced older public administration programs and treated the curricula of these older programs dismissively. I touch briefly on this phenomenon in chapter 21.

20. Jos C. N. Raadschelders and Kwang-Hoon Lee, "Trends in the Study of Public Administration: Empirical and Qualitative Observations from Public Administration Review, 2000–2009," *Public Administration Review* 71, no. 1 (2011): 19–33, 27; Chaoqun Ni, Cassidy R. Sugimoto, and Alice Robbin, "Examining the Evolution of the Field of Public Administration through a Bibliometric Analysis of Public Administration Review," *Public Administration Review* 77, no. 4 (2017): 496–509, 501.

21. Generally, see James J. Sheehan, *The Monopoly of Violence: Why Europeans Hate Going to War* (London: Faber & Faber, 2008).

22. Raadschelders and Lee, "Trends in the Study of Public Administration," 28–29.

23. H. Brinton Milward et al., "Is Public Management Neglecting the State?," *Governance* 29, no. 3 (2016): 1–26, 312. Also see the contributions of other authors to this roundtable.

24. Robert Durant and David Rosenbloom, "The Hollowing of American Public Administration," *American Review of Public Administration* 47, no. 7 (2016): 719–736, 725.

25. Jocelyne Bourgon, "Rethink, Reframe and Reinvent: Serving in the Twenty-First Century," *International Review of Administrative Sciences* 83, no. 4 (2017): 624–635, 633.

26. Christopher Pollitt, "Losing the Big Picture, and Influence Too," April 27, 2016, https://statecrafting.net/losing-the-big-picture-and-losing-influence-too-f4a2d8e57532. Similarly, see B. Guy Peters and Jon Pierre, "Two Roads to Nowhere: Appraising 30 Years of Public Administration Research," *Governance* 30, no. 1 (2016): 11–16, 11; Christopher Pollitt and Geert Bouckaert, *Public Management Reform: A Comparative Analysis*, 4th ed. (Oxford: Oxford University Press, 2017), 223–225.

27. Pollitt calls these megatrends: Christopher Pollitt, *Advanced Introduction to Public Management and Administration* (Northampton, MA: Edward Elgar, 2016), chap. 6; Christopher Pollitt, "Public Administration Research since 1980: Slipping Away from the Real World," *International Journal of Public Sector Management* 30, no. 6/7(2017): 255–265; Pollitt and Bouckaert, *Public Management Reform*, 224. I have called them "large forces": Alasdair Roberts, *Large Forces: What's Missing in Public Administration* (North Charleston, SC: CreateSpace, 2013). Donald Kettl has called them "the big trends shaping

the world of governance": Milward et al., "Is Public Management Neglecting the State?," 330.

28. Pollitt, "Public Administration Research since 1980," 3–4. Other important megatrends include shifts in power within the international system of states and the transformation of national economies.

29. Donald Kettl, *Escaping Jurassic Government* (Washington, DC: Brookings Institution, 2016), 180.

30. Ibid., 1.

31. Generally, see: Thomas E. Mann and Norman J. Ornstein, *The Broken Branch: How Congress Is Failing America* (New York: Oxford University Press, 2006); Thomas E. Mann and Norman J. Ornstein, *It's Even Worse Than It Looks* (New York: Basic Books, 2013).

32. Jonathan Rauch, *Demosclerosis* (New York: Times, 1994); Charles Murray, "Curing American Sclerosis," *American Criterion*, 33, no. 10 (2015): 4–8; Lawrence Jacobs and Desmond King, "America's Political Crisis: The Unsustainable State in a Time of Unraveling," *PS: Political Science and Politics* 42, no. 2 (2009): 277–285.

33. William Galston, "Intelligent Design," *American Interest* 3, no. 3 (2009): 6–12.

34. Francis Fukuyama, *Political Order and Political Decay* (New York: Farrar, Straus & Giroux, 2014), chap. 36; Francis Fukuyama, "America in Decay," *Foreign Affairs* 93, no. 5 (2014): 3–26.

35. Kettl, *Escaping Jurassic Government*, 2–3.

36. Sergio Fernandez and Hal G. Rainey, "Managing Successful Organizational Change in the Public Sector," *Public Administration Review* 66, no. 2 (2006): 168–176.

37. Christopher Pollitt, *Time, Policy, Management: Governing with the Past* (New York: Oxford University Press, 2008), 29; Jos C. N. Raadschelders, "Is American Public Administration Detached from Historical Context?," *American Review of Public Administration* 40, no. 3 (2010): 235–260, 235, and 241.

38. Raadschelders and Lee, "Trends in the Study of Public Administration," 19.

39. The label was coined by Christopher Hood: Christopher Hood, "A Public Management for All Seasons?," *Public Administration* 69, no. 1 (1991): 3–20.

40. David Osborne and Ted Gaebler, *Reinventing Government* (New York: Plume, 1992), 328; Donald Kettl, *The Global Public Management Revolution* (Washington, DC: Brookings Institution, 2005); Richard M. Walker, "Globalized Public Management: An Interdisciplinary Design Science?," *Journal of Public Administration Research and Theory* 21,suppl. 1 (2011): i53–i59, i55; Stella Z. Theodoulou and Ravi K. Roy, *Public Administration: A Very Short Introduction* (Oxford: Oxford University Press, 2016), chap. 5.

41. Opening address to the Global Forum on Reinventing Government, January 14, 1999, available online at https://www.c-span.org/video/?118369-1/global-forum-reinventing-government.

42. Francis Fukuyama, "The End of History?," *National Interest* 16, no. 3 (1989): 3–16.

43. John Williamson, "What Should the World Bank Think about the Washington Consensus?," *World Bank Research Observer* 15, no. 2 (2000): 251–264, 252–253.

44. Ali Farazmand, "The Future of Public Administration: Challenges and Opportunities," *Administration & Society* 44, no. 4 (2012): 487–517, 497.

45. Christopher Hood, *The Art of the State* (New York: Clarendon, 1998), chap. 9; Lynn, *Public Management*, chap. 2; Pollitt and Bouckaert, *Public Management Reform*, 11–15.

46. Yilin Hou et al., "The Case for Public Administration with a Global Perspective," *Journal of Public Administration Research and Theory* 21, suppl. 1 (2011): i45–i51, i46; Jody Fitzpatrick et al., "A New Look at Comparative Public Administration," *Public Administration Review* 71, no. 6 (2011): 821–830, 827; Kim Moloney and Nilima Gulrajani, "Globalized World, Globalized Research, Version 20.20," *Public Administration Review* 70 (2010): s298–s299; M. Shamsul Haque and Mark Turner, "Knowledge-Building in Asian Public Administration," *Public Administration and Development* 33, no. 4 (2013): 243–248.

47. Walker, "Globalized Public Management," i55–i56; Fernando Juliani and Otávio José de Oliveira, "State of Research on Public Service Management," *International Journal of Information Management* 36, no. 6, part A (2016): 1033–1041, 1036; M. Shamsul Haque, "Public Administration in a Globalized Asia," *Public Administration and Development* 33 (2013): 262–274, 271.

48. Haque and Turner, "Knowledge-Building in Asian Public Administration," 244.

49. Generally, see: Chalmers Johnson, *MITI and the Japanese Miracle: The Growth of Industrial Policy, 1925–1975* (Stanford, CA: Stanford University Press, 1982).

Anthony B.L. Cheung, "The Politics of Administrative Reforms in Asia: Paradigms and Legacies, Paths and Diversities," *Governance* 18, no. 2 (2005): 257–282, 263–264.

50. Generally, see: Ha-Joon Chang, *Bad Samaritans* (New York: Bloomsbury, 2008).

51. This interpretation is discussed extensively in Joseph Nye Jr., Philip Zelikow, and David King, eds., *Why People Don't Trust Government* (Cambridge, MA: Harvard University Press, 1997).

52. The Gallup World Poll, Edelman Trust Barometer, and Pew Research Center Global Attitudes surveys all show very high levels of trust for several Asian countries.

53. Dahai Zhao and Wei Hu, "Determinants of Public Trust in Government: Empirical Evidence from Urban China," *International Review of Administrative Sciences* 83, no. 2 (2017): 358–377.

54. OECD, *The State of the Public Service* (Paris: OECD Working Party on Public Employment and Management, 2008), chap. 2.

55. For example, the Indian Administrative Service has been described as the "steel frame" of government: Beryl Radin, "The Indian Administrative Service in the 21st Century," *International Journal of Public Administration* 30, no. 12–14 (2007): 1525–1548.

56. Geoffrey Shepherd, *Civil Service Reform in Developing Countries: Why Is It Going Badly?* (Washington, DC: World Bank, 2003), 12.

57. Alfred Tat-Kei Ho and Tobin Im, "Challenges in Building Effective and Competitive Government in Developing Countries," *American Review of Public Administration* 45, no. 3 (2015): 263–280, 276.

58. Gerald E. Caiden and Pachampet Sundaram, "The Specificity of Public Service Reform," *Public Administration and Development* 24, no. 5 (2004): 373–383, 373.

59. Ramanie Samaratunge, Quamrul Alam, and Julian Teicher, "The New Public Management Reforms in Asia: A Comparison of South and Southeast Asian Countries,"

International Review of Administrative Sciences 74, no. 1 (2008): 25–46, 25. The importance of various "contextual factors" is also discussed in Myung-Jae Moon and Patricia Ingraham, "Shaping Administrative Reform and Governance: An Examination of the Political Nexus Triads in Three Asian Countries," *Governance* 11, no. 1 (1998): 77–100; Suleyman Sozen and Ian Shaw, "The International Applicability of 'New' Public Management," *International Journal of Public Sector Management* 15, no. 6 (2002): 475–486, 483; Anthony Cheung, "The Politics of New Public Management: Some Experience from Reforms in East Asia," in *New Public Management: Current Trends and Future Prospects*, ed. Kate McLaughlin, Stephen Osborne, and Ewan Ferlie (London: Routledge, 2002), 243–273, 246; M. Shamsul Haque, "Global Rise of the Neoliberal State and Its Impact on Citizenship," *Asian Journal of Social Science* 36 (2008): 11–34, 28; Anthony Cheung and Ian Scott, *Governance and Public Sector Reform in Asia: Paradigm Shifts or Business as Usual?* (New York: Routledge Curzon, 2003); Cheung, "Politics of Administrative Reforms in Asia," 273; Martin Painter and B. Guy Peters, *Tradition and Public Administration* (London: Palgrave Macmillan, 2010), 3; Bidhya Bowornwathana, "Governance Reform Outcomes through Cultural Lens: Thailand," in *Cultural Aspects of Public Management Reform*, ed. Kuno Schedler and Isabella Proeller (Oxford: JAI, 2007), 275–298; Soma Pillay, "A Cultural Ecology of New Public Management," *International Review of Administrative Sciences* 74, no. 3 (2008): 373–394; Tobin Im, Jesse W. Campbell, and Seyeong Cha, "Revisiting Confucian Bureaucracy: Roots of the Korean Government's Culture and Competitiveness," *Public Administration and Development* 33, no. 4 (2013): 286–296; and Yulian Wihantoro et al., "Bureaucratic Reform in Post-Asian Crisis Indonesia: The Directorate General of Tax," *Critical Perspectives on Accounting* 31 (2015): 44–63.

60. Hughes, *Public Management and Administration*, 232–235; Abu Sarker, "New Public Management in Developing Countries," *International Journal of Public Sector Management* 19, no. 2 (2006): 180–203; Lan Xue and Kaibin Zhong, "Domestic Reform and Global Integration: Public Administration Reform in China over the Last 30 Years," *International Review of Administrative Sciences* 78, no. 2 (2012): 284–304, 288–289.

61. Cheung, "Politics of New Public Management," 245.

62. Cheung and Scott, *Governance and Public Sector Reform in Asia*, 2.

63. Tobin Im, *The Experience of Democracy and Bureaucracy in South Korea* (United Kingdom: Emerald, 2017), xvi–xxxviii.

64. Xue and Zhong, "Domestic Reform and Global Integration," 297–298. For further discussion about the importance of leaders' predispositions in the Asian context, see Jeffrey Straussman and Mengzhong Zhang, "Chinese Administrative Reforms in International Perspective," *International Journal of Public Sector Management* 14, no. 4 (2001): 411–422, 420; Caiden and Sundaram, "Specificity of Public Service Reform," 375; Bidhya Bowornwathana, "Thaksin's Model of Government Reform," *Asian Journal of Political Science* 12, no. 1 (2004): 135–152; Bidhya Bowornwathana, "Administrative Reform and Tidal Waves from Regime Shifts," *Asia Pacific Journal of Public Administration* 27, no. 1 (2005): 37–52; Tom Christensen, Dong Lisheng, and Martin Painter, "Administrative Reform in China's Central Government—How Much 'Learning from the West'?," *International Review of Administrative Sciences* 74, no. 3 (2008): 351–371, 362; and Cheung, "Politics of Administrative Reforms in Asia," 265.

65. Concern that the "publication preferences" of leading journals will lead to the neglect of "big problems" is also noted by Wei Zhang, Xiaolin Xu, Richard Evans, and Feng Yang, "Towards Internationalization: A Critical Assessment of China's Public Administration Research in a Global Context 2000–2014," *International Public Management Journal* 21, no. 1 (2018): 74–104, 97.

66. OECD, *Supporting Statebuilding in Situations of Conflict and Fragility* (Paris: OECD, 2011), 11.

67. The World Bank stopped distinguishing between developed and developing countries in 2016.However, the International Monetary Fund continues to distinguish between advanced economies and emerging and developing economies. Out of the 30 advanced economies included in the 2018 assessment of state fragility by the Fund for Peace, 28 were rated as stable or better. Out of the 142 emerging and developing economies, only 27 were rated as stable or better.

68. In general, see Robert I. Rotberg, *When States Fail: Causes and Consequences* (Princeton, NJ: Princeton University Press, 2004); Derick W. Brinkerhoff, *Governance in Post-Conflict Societies: Rebuilding Fragile States* (New York: Routledge, 2007); Lothar Brock, *Fragile States: Violence and the Failure of Intervention* (Cambridge: Polity, 2012); Brennan Kraxberger, *Failed States: Realities, Risks, and Responses* (North Charleston, SC: CreateSpace, 2012); Timothy D. Sisk, *Statebuilding: Consolidating Peace after Civil War* (Cambridge: Polity, 2013); and David Chandler and Timothy D. Sisk, *Routledge Handbook of International Statebuilding* (New York: Routledge, 2013).

69. Zoe Scott, *Literature Review on State-Building* (Birmingham, UK: Governance and Social Development Resource Centre, 2007), 3. The *Journal of Intervention and Statebuilding* was launched in 2007. Research on statebuilding also tends to be published in journals specializing in development policy or international relations, most notably *Third World Quarterly*, *Journal of International Development*, *International Peacekeeping*, *World Politics*, and *Global Governance*.

70. Derick W. Brinkerhoff, "Introduction," in *Governance in Post-Conflict Societies*, ed. Derick W. Brinkerhoff (New York: Routledge, 2007), 1–22, 1.

71. Sisk, *Statebuilding*, 175–176.

72. Sixty-six states were put in the categories of "high warning" or worse: Fund for Peace, *Fragile States Index* (Washington, DC: Fund for Peace, 2017), 6–7.

73. World Bank, *World Development Report 2011: Conflict, Security, and Development* (Washington, DC: World Bank, 2011), 2.

74. Fund for Peace, *Fragile States Index*, 26.

75. Rotberg, *When States Fail*, chap. 1; Ashraf Ghani and Clare Lockhart, *Fixing Failed States: A Framework for Rebuilding a Fractured World* (New York: Oxford University Press, 2008), chap. 7; Sisk, *Statebuilding*, 167–168; Clare Lockhart, "Sovereignty Strategies: Enhancing Core Governance Functions as a Post-Conflict and Conflict-Prevention Measure," *Daedalus* 147 (Winter 2018): 90–103.

76. Toby Dodge, "Intervention and Dreams of Exogenous Statebuilding: The Application of Liberal Peacebuilding in Afghanistan and Iraq," *Review of International Studies* 39, no. 5 (2013): 1189–1212, 1210. See also Catherine Goetze and Dejan Guzina, "Peacebuilding, Statebuilding, Nationbuilding—Turtles All the Way Down?," *Civil Wars* 10, no. 4 (2008): 319–347, 326–327, and 338–341; Brinkerhoff, "Introduction," 15–16.

77. Merriam, *Systematic Politics*, 32.

78. Previous works that have called explicitly for a macro perspective include Alasdair Roberts, "The Path Not Taken: Leonard White and the Macrodynamics of Administrative Development," *Public Administration Review* 69, no. 4 (2009): 764–775, 765; Ali Farazmand, "Building Administrative Capacity for the Age of Rapid Globalization," *Public Administration Review* 69, no. 6 (2009): 1007–1020, 1008; Robert F. Durant, "Parsimony, 'Error' Terms, and the Future of a Field," *Public Administration Review* 70 (2010): s319–s320, s320; Raadschelders and Lee, "Trends in the Study of Public Administration," 28–29; Durant and Rosenbloom, "Hollowing of American Public Administration," 9–10; and William Resh, "Thinking Institutionally Again About Public Administration," concept paper for the fiftieth anniversary of the Minnowbrook Conference(Los Angeles, CA: University of Southern California, August 2018).

79. Stephan Grimmelikhuijsen, Sebastian Jilke, Asmus Leth Olsen, and Lars Tummers, "Behavioral Public Administration: Combining Insights from Public Administration and Psychology," *Public Administration Review* 77 no. 1 (2017): 45–56, 46.See also Lars Tummers, Asmus Leth Olsen, Sebastian Jilke, and Stephan Grimmelikhuijsen, "Introduction to the Virtual Issue on Behavioral Public Administration," *Journal of Public Administration Research and Theory* (Special Issue, 2016): 1–3.

80. The danger of a "schism" among researchers is suggested by: Donald Moynihan, "A Great Schism Approaching? Towards a Micro and Macro Public Administration," *Journal of Behavioral Public Administration* 1 no. 1 (2018): 1–8.

81. The micro-meso-macro distinction is also recognized by Doug McTaggart and Janine O'Flynn: "Public Sector Reform," *Australian Journal of Public Administration* 74 no. 1 (2015): 13–22.

82. For example, see Mark H. Moore, "Policy Managers Need Policy Analysts," *Journal of Policy Analysis and Management* 1, no. 3 (1982): 413–418; Mark Moore, "A Conception of Public Management," in *Teaching Public Management: Proceedings of a Workshop to Assess Materials and Strategies for Teaching Public Management, Seattle, May 9–11, 1984* (Boston: Boston University Public Policy and Management Program, 1984), 1–12; E. Sam Overman, "Public Management: What's New and Different?," *Public Administration Review* 44, no. 3 (1984): 275–278, 278; Richard F. Elmore, "Graduate Education in Public Management: Working the Seams of Government," *Journal of Policy Analysis and Management* 6, no. 1 (1986): 69–83, 69–73; and Lynn, "Public Management," 172–182.

83. In 1984, E. Sam Overman observed that "Public management, 1980 style, is an amorphous aggregation of synthesizers and restaters"; Overman, "Public Management: What's New and Different?," 278. For example, the concept of corporate strategy developed at Harvard Business School was transmuted into the "strategic triangle" of the Harvard Kennedy School.

84. For an illustration of the early discussions over how the public management approach should influence the research agenda, see Lynn, "Public Management." Regarding graduate education, see Douglas T. Yates, "The Mission of Public Policy Programs: A Report on Recent Experience," *Policy Sciences* 8, no. 3 (1977): 363–373, and Elmore, "Graduate Education in Public Management." Regarding professional practice, see Joseph L. Bower, "Effective Public Management," *Harvard Business Review* 55, no. 2 (1977): 131–140; Gordon Chase, ed., *Bromides for Public Managers* (Cambridge, MA: Kennedy

School of Government,1980); Laurence E. Lynn, *Managing the Public's Business: The Job of the Government Executive* (New York: Basic Books, 1981); Moore, "Policy Managers Need Policy Analysts"; and Gordon Chase and Elizabeth C. Reveal, *How to Manage in the Public Sector* (Reading, MA: Addison-Wesley, 1983).

2. Acknowledging the State

1. Michael Goodhart, "Democratic Accountability in Global Politics: Norms, Not Agents," *Journal of Politics* 73, no. 1 (2011): 45–60, 49–50.
2. Colin Hay, Michael Lister, and David Marsh, *The State: Theories and Issues* (New York: Palgrave Macmillan, 2006), 1.
3. Anthony Giddens, *The Nation-State and Violence* (Chicester, UK: Wiley, 2013), 120.
4. Andrew Sobel, *International Political Economy in Context: Individual Choices, Global Effects* (Thousand Oaks, CA: CQ, 2013), 56.
5. Joe Painter and Alexander Sam Jeffrey, *Political Geography: An Introduction to Space and Power* (London: Sage, 2009), 20.
6. Vaughan Lowe, *International Law: A Very Short Introduction* (Oxford: Oxford University Press, 2015), 4.
7. Woodrow Wilson, "The Study of Administration," *Political Science Quarterly*, 2, no. 2 (1987): 201. On this as the "founding manifesto," see Raymond Seidelman, *Disenchanted Realists: Political Science and the American Crisis*, 2nd ed. (Albany: State University of New York Press, 2015), 266.
8. Marshall E. Dimock, "The Study of Administration," *American Political Science Review* 31, no. 1 (1937): 28–40, 31.
9. Max Weber, *From Max Weber: Essays in Sociology* (New York: Oxford University Press, 1946), 78.
10. John A. Hall and G. John Ikenberry, *The State* (Minneapolis: University of Minnesota Press, 1989), 1–2.
11. John L. Campbell and John A. Hall, *The World of States* (London: Bloomsbury, 2015), 4.
12. Colin Hay and Michael Lister, "Introduction: Theories of the State," in *The State: Theories and Issues*, ed. Colin Hay, David Lister, and David March (New York: Palgrave Macmillan, 2006), 1–20, 5; Bob Jessop, *The State: Past, Present, Future* (New York: Polity, 2016), 49.
13. S. E. Finer, *The History of Government from the Earliest Times*, 3 vols. (New York: Oxford University Press, 1997), 1–2.
14. Theda Skocpol, *States and Social Revolutions* (New York: Cambridge University Press, 1979), 29. Similarly, see Michael Mann, *States, War, and Capitalism: Studies in Political Sociology* (New York: Basil Blackwell, 1988), 4.
15. For a discussion of the concept with regard to political institutions, see Bruce Gilley, *The Right to Rule: How States Win and Lose Legitimacy* (New York: Columbia University Press, 2009), 3–16. For a more abstract definition, see Mark C. Suchman, "Managing Legitimacy: Strategic and Institutional Approaches," *Academy of Management Review* 20, no. 3 (1995): 571–610, 574.

16. "As the chief of the East German security services noted to Erich Honecker in 1989, 'we can't beat hundreds of thousands of people'": Vladimir Gel'man, *Authoritarian Russia: Analyzing Post-Soviet Regime Changes* (Pittsburgh, PA: University of Pittsburgh Press, 2015), 144.

17. Hersch Lauterpacht, *Recognition in International Law* (Cambridge: Cambridge University Press, 1947), 28.

18. S. E. Finer, *Comparative Government* (Harmondsworth, UK: Penguin, 1974), 30.

19. Carma Hogue, *Government Organization Summary Report* (Washington, DC: United States Census Bureau, 2013), 1.

20. "Free institutions are next to impossible in a country made up of different nationalities. Among a people without fellow-feeling, especially if they read and speak different languages, the united public opinion, necessary to the working of representative government, cannot exist": John Stuart Mill, *Considerations on Representative Government* (London: Parker, Son, & Bourn, 1861), 289.

3. States and Societies

1. Malcolm N. Shaw, *International Law* (New York: Cambridge University Press, 2008), 211–213, 1138–1140.

2. Vaughan Lowe, *International Law: A Very Short Introduction* (Oxford: Oxford University Press, 2015), 4.

3. Shaw, *International Law*, 487.

4. Niccolò Machiavelli, *The Essential Writings of Machiavelli* (New York: Modern Library, 2007), 72.

5. Some scholars insist on a distinction between the system and society of states: Adam Watson, "Systems of States," *Review of International Studies* 16, no. 2 (1990): 99–109. This distinction is not as tenable today as it might have been in previous centuries.

6. Hedley Bull, *The Anarchical Society: A Study of Order in World Politics*, 3rd ed. (New York: Columbia University Press, 2002), 44–49.

7. Herbert Butterfield, *Christianity and History* (London: Collins/Fontana, 1957), 119–120.

8. Christopher Dawson, *The Dividing of Christendom* (New York: Sheed & Ward, 1965), 38–39.

9. Although there are still some city-states, such as Singapore and Monaco, today.

4. Leaders and Their Goals

1. "[All states] are ruled by a group of influential individuals who are less numerous than those that they govern": S. E. Finer, *Comparative Government* (Harmondsworth, UK: Penguin, 1974), 39.

2. Woodrow Wilson, *The State: Elements of Historical and Practical Politics* (Boston: D. C. Heath, 1889), 593–594.

3. Vincent Sheean, *Mahatma Gandhi: A Great Life in Brief* (New York, Knopf, 1955), 32.

4. C. Wright Mills, *The Power Elite* (New York: Oxford University Press, 1999). Similarly, see Harold Joseph Laski, *Authority in the Modern State* (New Haven, CT: Yale University Press, 1919), 27.

5. Ronald E. Robinson and John Gallagher, *Africa and the Victorians* (New York: St. Martin's Press, 1961), 20. A similar notion is that of political mind: "patterns of thought, ways of perceiving the world, psychological attitudes, ideological premises, and working theories," that relate to both domestic and foreign affairs and are shared by a ruling group: Robert C. Tucker, *The Soviet Political Mind* (New York: Norton, 1971), ix.

6. Marshall E. Dimock, "The Objectives of Governmental Reorganization," *Public Administration Review* 11, no. 4 (1951): 233–241, 234.

7. Leonard D. White, *Introduction to the Study of Public Administration*, 3d ed. (New York: Macmillan, 1948), viii; White, *Introduction to the Study of Public Administration*, 7.

8. White, *Introduction to the Study of Public Administration*, 7.

9. Charles E. Merriam, "The Ends of Government," *American Political Science Review* 38, no. 1 (1944): 21.

10. Ashraf Ghani and Clare Lockhart, *Fixing Failed States: A Framework for Rebuilding a Fractured World* (New York: Oxford University Press, 2008), chap. 7. For other statements of goals, see Robert I. Rotberg, *When States Fail: Causes and Consequences* (Princeton, NJ: Princeton University Press, 2004), chap. 1; OECD, *Concepts and Dilemmas of State Building in Fragile Situations* (Paris: OECD, 2008), 16; OECD, *Supporting Statebuilding in Situations of Conflict and Fragility* (Paris: OECD, 2011), 21–22; and Timothy D. Sisk, *Statebuilding: Consolidating Peace after Civil War* (Cambridge: Polity, 2013), 167–168. As the OECD text suggests, assumptions about goals are embedded in the very definition of fragile states: by inverting the definition of fragility, we obtain a statement of goals. With this in mind, see David Chandler and Timothy D. Sisk, *Routledge Handbook of International Statebuilding* (New York: Routledge, 2013), xx–xxii.

11. Bruce Bueno de Mesquita, *The Logic of Political Survival* (Cambridge, MA: MIT Press, 2003), 8–9. See also Barry Ames, *Political Survival: Politicians and Public Policy in Latin America* (Berkeley: University of California Press, 1987), 7; Peter Trubowitz, *Politics and Strategy: Partisan Ambition and American Statecraft* (Princeton, NJ: Princeton University Press, 2011), 4; and Vladimir Gel'man, *Authoritarian Russia: Analyzing Post-Soviet Regime Changes* (Pittsburgh, PA: University of Pittsburgh Press, 2015), 5.

12. James Crawford, *The Creation of States in International Law* (New York: Oxford University Press, 2006), 58.

13. James C. Scott, *Seeing Like a State* (New Haven, CT: Yale University Press, 1998), 1–5.

14. "It is profitless to look for criteria for the legitimacy of political regimes that apply in all historical circumstances.... [There can be no] universal theory of political legitimacy": John Gray, *Two Faces of Liberalism* (New York, The New Press, 2000), 106.

15. Joseph S. Nye, *The Future of Power* (New York: Public Affairs, 2011), chap. 4.

16. A critical history of the concept of human rights is provided by Samuel Moyn: *Human Rights and the Uses of History* (New York, Verso, 2017).

17. Article 21(3), Universal Declaration of Human Rights, https://www.ohchr.org/en/udhr/pages/udhrindex.aspx. See also Jack Donnelly, *Universal Human Rights in Theory and Practice*, 3rd ed. (Ithaca, NY: Cornell University Press, 2013), chap. 13.

18. Giovanni Botero, *The Reason of State* (London: Routledge & K. Paul, 1956), 3.

19. "Renaissance Italy was a dangerous place, and a ruler who wanted to preserve and extend his stato, and to deal with other similar statos around him, had to be guided not by standards of right and wrong but by cool calculation of what was expedient. This calculation was called *ragione di stato*, reason of state": Adam Watson, *The Evolution of International Society: A Comparative Historical Analysis* (London: Routledge, 2009), 5. See also Michel Foucault, *Security, Territory, Population: Lectures at the Collège de France, 1977–78* (Basingstoke, UK: Palgrave Macmillan, 2007), 255–310.

20. For an earlier attempt to revive the concept of statecraft within the field of policy analysis and management, see generally Charles W. Anderson, *Statecraft: An Introduction to Political Choice and Judgment* (New York: Wiley, 1977).

21. Chandler and Sisk, *Routledge Handbook of International Statebuilding*, 393–394. Also see the many other references to the "moral and political tradeoffs" of statebuilding in this volume and in other books on the subject.

22. Merilee S. Grindle, "Good Enough Governance: Poverty Reduction and Reform in Developing Countries," *Governance* 17, no. 4 (2004): 525–548, 526.

23. Jeff Goodell, "Obama Takes On Climate Change," *Rolling Stone*, October 6, 2015, 36–45.

5. Strategies for Governing

1. William A. Williams defined a way of life as "the combination of patterns and thought that . . . defines the thrust and character" of a society: *Empire As a Way of Life* (New York: Oxford University Press, 1980), 12. A durable strategy for governing is one that is embedded in these "patterns of thought"—that is, popular culture as well as the design of institutions.

2. Steven E. Schier, *Transforming America: Barack Obama in the White House* (Lanham, MD: Rowman & Littlefield, 2011), 39.

3. For a discussion of the "Washington Consensus" by the man who coined the phrase, see: John Williamson, "What Should the World Bank Think about the Washington Consensus?," *World Bank Research Observer* 15, no. 2 (2000).

4. Executive Office of the President, *National Security Strategy of the United States* (Washington, DC: Executive Office of the President, 2002), iv.

5. I have borrowed the language of Laurence E. Lynn Jr. Lynn discusses this perception about global trends but rejects this view himself: Carolyn J. Hill and Laurence E. Lynn Jr., *Public Management: Thinking and Acting in Three Dimensions*, 2nd ed. (Los Angeles: Sage, 2016), 2. For articulations of this view about global convergence, see David Osborne and Ted Gaebler, *Reinventing Government* (New York: Plume, 1992), 328; Donald Kettl, *The Global Public Management Revolution* (Washington, DC: Brookings Institution, 2005), 1-6; Richard M. Walker, "Globalized Public Management: An Interdisciplinary Design Science?," *Journal of Public Administration Research and Theory* 21,

suppl. 1 (2011): i53-i59; and Stella Z. Theodoulou and Ravi K. Roy, *Public Administration: A Very Short Introduction* (Oxford: Oxford University Press, 2016), chap. 5.

6. Generally, see Richard McGregor, *The Party: The Secret World of China's Communist Rulers* (New York: Harper, 2010); Wei-Wei Zhang, *The China Wave: Rise of a Civilizational State* (Hackensack, NJ: World Century, 2012); Orville Schell and John Delury, *Wealth and Power: China's Long March to the Twenty-First Century* (New York: Random House, 2013); Daniel Bell, *The China Model: Political Meritocracy and the Limits of Democracy* (Princeton, NJ: Princeton University Press, 2015); Stein Ringen, *The Perfect Dictatorship: China in the 21st Century* (Hong Kong: Hong Kong University Press, 2016); Joshua Kurlantzick, *State Capitalism: How the Return of Statism Is Transforming the World* (New York: Oxford University Press, 2016); and Howard W. French, *Everything under the Heavens: How the Past Helps Shape China's Push for Global Power* (New York: Alfred A. Knopf, 2017).

7. Pew Global Indicators Database, "How Satisfied Are You with the Country's Direction?," accessed March 15, 2019: http://www.pewglobal.org/database/indicator/3/survey/all/.

8. Anastasia Borik, "Can Russia and the West Reconcile through Counter-Terrorism?," *Russia Direct*, July 2, 2015, http://www.russia-direct.org/analysis/can-russia-and-west-reconcile-through-counter-terrorism. Vladimir Putin has also rejected the "standardized model" in speeches.

9. Generally, see Karen Dawisha, *Putin's Kleptocracy: Who Owns Russia?* paperback ed. (New York: Simon & Schuster, 2015); Vladimir Gel′man, *Authoritarian Russia: Analyzing Post-Soviet Regime Changes* (Pittsburgh, PA: University of Pittsburgh Press, 2015); Bobo Lo, *Russia and the New World Disorder* (Washington, DC: Brookings Institution Press, 2015); Walter Laqueur, *Putinism: Russia and Its Future with the West* (New York: Thomas Dunne, 2015); and Arkady Ostrovsky, *The Invention of Russia: The Journey from Gorbachev's Freedom to Putin's War* (London: Atlantic, 2015).

10. B. Michael Frolic, "Reflections on the Chinese Model of Development," *Social Forces* 57, no. 2 (1978): 384–418. There is substantial change even in more recent history. "Most leaders of the Chinese Communist Party acknowledge their political structure to be a developing story. Every reform administration has been drastically different from its predecessor": William Overholt, *China's Crisis of Success* (New York, NY: Cambridge University Press, 2018), 262.

11. Edward Luttwak, writing about the related concept of grand strategy, has observed that "all countries have grand strategies, whether they know it or not": Edward Luttwak, *The Grand Strategy of the Byzantine Empire* (Cambridge, MA: Belknap, 2009), 409.

12. Kevin Narizny makes the same point about grand strategy: Kevin Narizny, *The Political Economy of Grand Strategy* (Ithaca, NY: Cornell University Press, 2007), 10.

13. Lukas Milevski, *The Evolution of Modern Grand Strategic Thought* (Oxford: Oxford University Press, 2016), 1. Milevski provides a history of the concept within international relations and security studies. Brief histories are also provided by Hal Brands, *What Good Is Grand Strategy? Power and Purpose in American Statecraft* (Ithaca, NY: Cornell University Press, 2014), 1–3, and William C. Martel, *Grand Strategy in Theory and Practice: The Need for an Effective American Foreign Policy* (New York: Cambridge

University Press, 2015), 24–26. There is also a similarity between this concept and the idea of the "public philosophy" described by Theodore Lowi and the "political formula" described by Gaetano Mosca: Theodore Lowi, "The Public Philosophy: Interest-Group Liberalism," *American Political Science Review* 61, no. 1 (1967): 5–24, 5; Gaetano Mosca, *The Ruling Class* (New York, McGraw-Hill, 1939), 70–71.

14. David Prescott Barrows, "Review of 'Grand Strategy' by H. A. Sargeaunt and G. West," *Annals of the American Academy of Political and Social Science* 221 (1942): 207–208, 207.

15. Basil Henry Liddell Hart, *The Strategy of Indirect Approach* (London: Faber & Faber, 1941), 10–11, 187–188, 202–205. See also Henry Antony Sargeaunt and Geoffrey West, *Grand Strategy* (New York: Thomas Y. Crowell, 1941), 7, 9, 215.

16. Edward Mead Earle, ed., *Makers of Modern Strategy* (Princeton NJ: Princeton University Press, 1943), viii.

17. Kennedy and Gaddis collaborated with Charles Hill to establish the Grand Strategy Program at Yale University. See Linda Kulman, *Teaching Common Sense: The Grand Strategy Program at Yale University* (New Haven, CT: Prospecta, 2016).

18. Paul M. Kennedy, *Grand Strategies in War and Peace* (New Haven, CT: Yale University Press, 1991), 4–6. Kennedy also relied on the concept of grand strategy in an influential 1987 book: Paul M. Kennedy, *The Rise and Fall of the Great Powers: Economic Change and Military Conflict from 1500 to 2000* (New York: Vintage, 1987).

19. John Lewis Gaddis, *What Is Grand Strategy?* (Durham, NC: Duke University, 2009), 7.

20. John Lewis Gaddis, "A Grand Strategy of Transformation," *Foreign Policy*, no. 133 (2002): 50–57; John Lewis Gaddis, *Surprise, Security, and the American Experience* (Cambridge, MA: Harvard University Press, 2004), 14; John Lewis Gaddis, *Strategies of Containment: A Critical Appraisal of American National Security Policy During the Cold War* (New York: Oxford University Press, 2005), Chapter 12; John Lewis Gaddis, *On Grand Strategy* (New York: Penguin Press, 2018), 21-22; Paul M. Kennedy, "American Grand Strategy, Today and Tomorrow," in *Grand Strategies in War and Peace*, ed. Paul M. Kennedy (New Haven, CT: Yale University Press, 1991), 167–184, 167, and 179–182.

21. Brands, *What Good Is Grand Strategy?*, 2–3. For a similar and more expansive explanation, see Hal Brands, *American Grand Strategy in the Age of Trump* (Washington, DC: Brookings Institution Press, 2018), viii–ix.

22. Edward Luttwak, *Strategy: The Logic of War and Peace* (Cambridge, MA: Belknap, 2001), 211.

23. Peter Trubowitz, *Politics and Strategy: Partisan Ambition and American Statecraft* (Princeton, NJ: Princeton University Press, 2011), 1 and 9.

24. In the 1970s, Henry Kissinger observed, "Israel has no foreign policy; only domestic politics." Edward Sheehan, "How Kissinger Did It: Step by Step in the Middle East," *Foreign Policy* 22 (Spring 1976): 3–70. Susan Shirk has observed, "Preoccupation with domestic politics is not unique to China's leaders. Even in Western democracies like our own, foreign policy is driven as much by domestic considerations as by the opinions of our allies and other foreign countries": Susan Shirk, *China: Fragile Superpower* (New York: Oxford University Press, 2007), 8. In 2018, a senior European policymaker observed

of President Trump that "nobody knows when Trump is doing international diplomacy and when he is doing election campaigning in Montana": David M. Herszenhorn and Jacopo Barigazzi, "Very Stable Trump? European Leaders Beg to Differ," *Politico*, July 12, 2018, https://www.politico.com/story/2018/07/12/donald-trump-behavior-nato-summit-europe-716035.

25. Ira Katznelson and Martin Shefter, *Shaped by War and Trade: International Influences on American Political Development* (Princeton, NJ: Princeton University Press, 2002), 4.

6. Factors and Forces

1. I review this literature more closely in Alasdair Roberts, *Large Forces: What's Missing in Public Administration* (North Charleston, SC: CreateSpace, 2013), chap. 2. In talking this way, scholars in the new field of public administration were following the example of Progressive Era historians like James Harvey Robinson and Frederick Jackson Turner: John Higham, *History: Professional Scholarship in America* (Baltimore: Johns Hopkins University Press, 1983), 113.

2. Luther H. Gulick, *Administrative Reflections from World War II* (University, AL: University of Alabama Press, 1948), 1.

3. Lynton K. Caldwell, "The Relevance of Administrative History," *International Review of Administrative Sciences* 21, no. 3 (1955): 461.

4. Robert A. Dahl, "The Science of Public Administration: Three Problems," *Public Administration Review* 7, no. 1 (1947): 1–11, 11.

5. Gaus, *Reflections on Public Administration* (University, AL: University of Alabama Press, 1947), 1–19. Gaus gave a shorter sketch of this approach in an earlier book: John M. Gaus, Leon O. Wolcott, and Verne B. Lewis, *Public Administration and the United States Department of Agriculture* (Chicago: Public Administration Service, 1940).

6. Leonard D. White, *Introduction to the Study of Public Administration*, 2nd ed. (New York: Macmillan, 1939), 18.

7. I discuss these books more fully in Alasdair Roberts, "The Path Not Taken: Leonard White and the Macrodynamics of Administrative Development," *Public Administration Review* 69, no. 4 (2009): 764–775.

8. Leonard D. White, *The Republican Era, 1869–1901: A Study in Administrative History* (New York: Macmillan, 1958), 1; Leonard D. White, *The Jeffersonians: A Study in Administrative History, 1801–1829* (New York: Macmillan, 1951), 5 and 131; Leonard D. White, *The Jacksonians: A Study in Administrative History, 1829–1861* (New York: Macmillan, 1954), 7, 48.

9. A more recent application of the "social forces" approach is offered by Judith Teichman, who observes that "powerful social forces may create, destroy and reconstitute institutions": Judith A. Teichman, *Social Forces and States: Poverty and Distributional Outcomes in South Korea, Chile, and Mexico* (Stanford, CA: Stanford University Press, 2012), 3.

10. Herbert Croly, *The Promise of American Life* (New York: Macmillan, 1909), 71.

11. One illustration: the inability of state authorities to "climb hills": James C. Scott, *The Art of Not Being Governed* (New Haven, CT: Yale University Press, 2009), 20. Another is the preference for decentralization in expansive states and empires, especially where communications are slow.

7. Laws, Organizations, Programs, and Practices

1. Charles W. Anderson, "Comparative Policy Analysis: The Design of Measures," *Comparative Politics* 4, no. 1 (1971): 117–131, 121.

2. Samuel P. Huntington, *Political Order in Changing Societies* (New Haven, CT: Yale University Press, 1968), 12.

3. James G. March and Johan P. Olsen, *Rediscovering Institutions: The Organizational Basis of Politics* (New York: The Free Press, 1989), 160.

4. Douglass C. North, *Institutions, Institutional Change, and Economic Performance* (New York: Cambridge University Press, 1990), 3.

5. James Mahoney and Kathleen Ann Thelen, eds., *Explaining Institutional Change: Ambiguity, Agency, and Power* (New York: Cambridge University Press, 2010), 4.

6. Robert E. Goodin, "Institutions and Their Design," in *The Theory of Institutional Design*, ed. Robert E. Goodin (New York: Cambridge University Press, 1996), 1–53, 21.

7. They may also be referred to simply as institutions, applying an older and narrower meaning of that word. For an attempt to distinguish between institutions and organizations, see North, *Institutions, Institutional Change, and Economic Performance*, 5.

8. Government Accountability Office, *A Glossary of Terms Used in the Federal Budget Process* (Washington, DC: Government Accountability Office, 2005), 79.

9. James A. Bill and Robert L. Hardgrave, *Comparative Politics: The Quest for Theory* (Washington, DC: University Press of America, 1981), 3. See also Harry Eckstein, "On the 'Science' of the State," *Daedalus* 108, no. 4 (1979): 1–20, 2–3.

10. Paul Johnson, *Stalin: The Kremlin Mountaineer* (Seattle, WA: Amazon, 2014), chap. 3.

11. Bernard Bailyn, *The Ideological Origins of the American Revolution* (Cambridge, MA: Belknap, 1992); J.A.W. Gunn, *Beyond Liberty and Property: The Process of Self-Recognition in Eighteenth-Century Political Thought* (Kingston, ON: McGill-Queen's University Press, 1983).

12. Walter Bagehot, *The English Constitution* (London: Chapman and Hall, 1867), 5 and 11.

13. Frank J. Goodnow, *Politics and Administration: A Study in Government* (New York: The Macmillan Company, 1900), v.

14. Anthony King, *Who Governs Britain?* (London: Pelican, 2015), vi. For two recent analyses that emphasize the distinction between appearances and realities, see Michael J. Glennon, *National Security and Double Government* (New York: Oxford University Press, 2015) and Mike Lofgren, *The Deep State: The Fall of the Constitution and the Rise of a Shadow Government* (New York: Viking, 2016).

8. Aspects of Institutional Stewardship

1. Elizabeth Sanders, describing the scope of the scholarly enterprise known as historical institutionalism (HI), employs a similar categorization. She says that HI is concerned with the "construction, maintenance, and adaptation of institutions": Elizabeth Sanders, "Historical Institutionalism," in *The Oxford Handbook of Political Institutions*, eds. R.A.W. Rhodes, Sarah A. Binder, and Bert Rockman (New York: Oxford University Press, 2006), 39–55, 42.

2. M.J.C. Vile, *Constitutionalism and the Separation of Powers*, 2nd ed. (Indianapolis: Liberty Fund, 1998), 29–32; Joerg Tremmel, "Parliaments and Future Generations: The Four-Power-Model," in *The Politics of Sustainability*, ed. Dieter Birnbacher and May Thorseth (London: Routledge, 2015), 212–233.

3. Timothy D. Sisk, *Statebuilding: Consolidating Peace after Civil War* (Cambridge: Polity, 2013), 65.

4. Samuel P. Huntington, *Political Order in Changing Societies* (New Haven, CT: Yale University Press, 1968), 12.

5. World Bank, *World Development Report 2017: Governance and the Law* (Washington, DC: World Bank, 2017), 5.

6. David Lake, *The Statebuilder's Dilemma* (Ithaca, NY: Cornell University Press, 2016), chap. 1.

7. Luther Gulick, "Notes on the Theory of Organization," in *Papers on the Science of Administration*, ed. Luther Gulick and L. Urwick (New York: Institute of Public Administration, 1937).

8. James Q. Wilson, *Bureaucracy: What Government Agencies Do and Why They Do It* (New York: Basic Books, 1989), 375.

9. Laurence E. Lynn Jr., *Public Management: Old and New* (New York: Routledge, 2006), 10; emphasis added.

10. William Overholt captures this idea when he observes that Asian states have been "forced to evolve in a shape-shifting manner" over the last half-century: William Overholt, *China's Crisis of Success* (New York, NY: Cambridge University Press, 2018), 240.

11. Letter from Thomas Jefferson to Samuel Kercheval, June 12, 1816. http://www.let.rug.nl/usa/presidents/thomas-jefferson/letters-of-thomas-jefferson/jefl246.php. Accessed March 16, 2019.

12. John Dewey, *The Public and Its Problems* (New York: H. Holt, 1927), chap. 1.

13. Robert M. MacIver, *The Modern State* (Oxford: Clarendon, 1926), vii.

14. MacIver, *The Web of Government* (New York: Macmillan, 1947), 269.

15. "A world of constant flux": Kennedy, "Grand Strategy in War and Peace: Toward a Broader Definition," in *Grand Strategies in War and Peace*, ed. Paul M. Kennedy (New Haven, CT: Yale University Press, 1991), 1–7, 7; "A state that ignores systemic pressures will not survive any more than a firm that persistently ignores market signals": Charles Jones, *International Relations: A Beginner's Guide* (London: Oneworld, 2014), 41.

16. Nicholas Spykman, *America's Strategy in World Politics: The United States and the Balance of Power* (New York: Harcourt Brace, 1942), 464–465. At about the same time, George F. Kennan wrote, "International political life is something organic, not something mechanical. Its essence is change; and the only systems for the regulation of international

life which can be effective over long periods of time are ones sufficiently subtle, sufficiently pliable, to adjust themselves to constant change in the interests and power of the various countries involved": George F. Kennan and Frank Costigliola, *The Kennan Diaries* (New York: W. W. Norton, 2014), 170.

17. For example, Michael Cox, Timothy Dunne, and Ken Booth, *Empires, Systems and States: Great Transformations in International Politics* (Cambridge: Cambridge University Press, 2001); Ken Booth, *International Relations in All That Matters* (London: Hodder & Stoughton, 2014), 25.

18. Charles B. Hagan, "Geopolitics," *Journal of Politics* 4, no. 4 (1942): 478–490, 484.

19. Arthur M. Schlesinger, *The Imperial Presidency* (Boston: Houghton Mifflin, 1973), 164.

20. James G. March and Johan P. Olsen, "The New Institutionalism: Organizational Factors in Political Life," *American Political Science Review* 78, no. 3 (1984): 734–749, 737.

21. J. G. March and Johan P. Olsen, "Elaborating the 'New Institutionalism,'" in *The Oxford Handbook of Political Institutions*, eds. R. A. W. Rhodes, Sarah A. Binder, and Bert Rockman (New York: Oxford University Press, 2006), 3–22, 6.

22. Francis Fukuyama, *The Origins of Political Order* (New York: Farrar, Straus & Giroux, 2011), 16.

23. Ibid., 16 and 40; Fukuyama, *Political Order and Political Decay*, 5, 439–444.

24. Mancur Olson, *The Rise and Decline of Nations* (New Haven, CT: Yale University Press, 1982), 77–78.

25. Jonathan Rauch, "Demosclerosis," *National Journal* (1992): 1998–2003.

26. For a more extensive discussion, see Alasdair Roberts, *Four Crises of American Democracy: Representation, Mastery, Discipline, Anticipation* (New York: Oxford University Press, 2017), chap. 6.

27. Arnold Toynbee and D. C. Somervell, *A Study of History* (New York: Oxford University Press, 1987), 4.

9. Challenges in Strategy-Making

1. Article 21, Universal Declaration of Human Rights. http://www.un.org/en/universal-declaration-human-rights. Accessed March 16, 2019.

2. Carl von Clausewitz, *On War*, 3 vols. (London: N. Trübner, 1873), 25. Also "The great uncertainty of all data in war is a peculiar difficulty, because all action must, to a certain extent, be planned in a mere twilight": Ibid., 54.

3. Henry Kissinger, *The Necessity for Choice: Prospects of American Foreign Policy* (London: Chatto & Windus, 1961), 355.

4. Susan Shirk, *China: Fragile Superpower* (New York: Oxford University Press, 2007), chap. 3; Orville Schell and John Delury, *Wealth and Power: China's Long March to the Twenty-First Century* (New York: Random House, 2013), chap. 12; David L. Shambaugh, *China's Future* (New York: Polity, 2016), chap. 3; and Howard W. French, *Everything under the Heavens: How the Past Helps Shape China's Push for Global Power* (New York: Alfred A. Knopf, 2017), chap. 1.

5. Niccolò Machiavelli, *The Prince* (Chicago: University of Chicago Press, 1985), chap. 17.

6. Donald S. Macdonald, *Thumper: The Memoirs of the Honourable Donald S. Macdonald* (Kingston, ON: McGill-Queen's University Press, 2014), 197–198.

7. Adolf A. Berle, *The 20th Century Capitalist Revolution* (New York: Harcourt, 1954), 11.

8. Theodore J. Lowi and Alan Stone, *Nationalizing Government: Public Policies in America* (Beverly Hills, CA: Sage, 1978), 440–441.

9. For discussion of the related concept of "policy legacies," see Peter B. Evans, Dietrich Rueschemeyer, and Theda Skocpol, *Bringing the State Back In* (New York: Cambridge University Press, 1985).

10. Marx continues, "Tradition from all the dead generations weighs like a nightmare on the brain of the living": Karl Marx, *Later Political Writings* (Cambridge: Cambridge University Press, 1996), 32.

11. James C. Scott discusses several of these failed reform projects in *Seeing Like a State*.

12. Joseph A. Schumpeter, *Capitalism, Socialism, and Democracy* (London: Allen & Unwin, 1976), chap. 7.

13. Martin V. Melosi, *Effluent America: Cities, Industry, Energy, and the Environment* (Pittsburgh, PA: University of Pittsburgh Press, 2001), 130.

14. For example, see Roger B. Porter, *Presidential Decision Making* (New York: Cambridge University Press, 1980).

15. Michael Barber, *Instruction to Deliver* (London: Politico, 2007), 297–300.

16. How Secretary of State Rex Tillerson is said to have described President Donald Trump in 2017. For this and other critical assessments of Trump's decision-making capacities, see Bob Woodward, *Fear: Trump in the White House* (Washington, DC: Simon and Schuster, 2018), 224, 227, 263, 285, and 307. Brian Rathbun argues that rationality in executive decision-making is in fact rare: Brian Rathbun, "The Rarity of Realpolitik: What Bismarck's Rationality Reveals About International Politics," *International Security* 43, no. 1 (2018), 7–55.

17. Daniel Bell, *The China Model: Political Meritocracy and the Limits of Democracy* (Princeton, NJ: Princeton University Press, 2015), 1–13.

10. The Struggle for Mastery

1. Bobo Lo, *Russia and the New World Disorder* (Washington, DC: Brookings Institution Press, 2015), 205.

2. James Bryce, *The American Commonwealth* (New York: Macmillan, 1914), 1:295.

3. Lippmann, *Drift and Mastery* (New York: Mitchell Kennerley, 1914), 64.

4. Ron Chernow, *Washington: A Life* (New York: Penguin, 2010), 19.

5. George Washington, *The Writings of George Washington*, 14 vols. (New York: G. P. Putnam's Sons, 1889), Vol. 2, 331.

6. We refer to these data as *statistics*: the word itself derives from the Latin term *statisticum*, which means "of the state."

7. Generally, see Clifford Siskin, *System: The Shaping of Modern Knowledge* (Cambridge, MA: MIT Press, 2016).

8. Peter Andreas, *Smuggler Nation: How Illicit Trade Made America* (New York: Oxford University Press, 2013), 75.

9. Daniel Okrent, *Last Call: The Rise and Fall of Prohibition* (New York: Scribner, 2010), 3 and 373; Albert E. Sawyer, "The Enforcement of National Prohibition," *Annals of the American Academy of Political and Social Science* 163 (1932): 10–29.

10. For a good exposition of difficulties with the "war on drugs," see Tom Wainwright, *Narconomics: How to Run a Drug Cartel* (New York: PublicAffairs, 2016).

11. Danger, Strategic Fragility, and Realism

1. Herbert Butterfield, *Christianity and History* (London: Collins/Fontana, 1957), 119–120.

2. For summaries of the realist approach in international relations, see Hedley Bull, *The Anarchical Society: A Study of Order in World Politics*, 3rd ed. (New York: Columbia University Press, 2002), 23–24; Michael Joseph Smith, *Realist Thought from Weber to Kissinger* (Baton Rouge: Louisiana State University Press, 1986), 1; and Jonathan Haslam, *No Virtue Like Necessity: Realist Thought in International Relations since Machiavelli* (New Haven, CT: Yale University Press, 2002), 12–13.

3. For defenses of Machiavelli, see Catherine H. Zuckert, *Machiavelli's Politics* (Chicago: University of Chicago Press, 2017); Erica Benner, *Be Like the Fox: Machiavelli in His World* (New York: W. W. Norton, 2017); and Maurizio Viroli, *How to Read Machiavelli* (London: Granta, 2008).

4. Niccolò Machiavelli, *The Essential Writings of Machiavelli* (New York: Modern Library, 2007), 72.

5. Jean Bodin, *Six Books of the Commonwealth* (New York: Barnes & Noble, 1967), Book 4.

6. Francis Bacon, *The Essays of Francis Bacon* (Boston: Houghton, 1908), 44–46.

7. The risks of factionalism, insurrection, and sedition are discussed throughout the Federalist and anti-Federalist papers. In particular, see Federalist no. 10: http://avalon.law.yale.edu/18th_century/fed10.asp. Accessed March 16, 2019.

8. Timothy D. Sisk, *Statebuilding: Consolidating Peace after Civil War* (Cambridge: Polity, 2013), chap. 1.

9. Paul Krugman, "Our Unknown Country," *New York Times*, November 8, 2016.

10. Paul Krugman, "How Republics End," *New York Times*, December 19, 2016.

11. Anthony King, *Who Governs Britain?* (London: Pelican, 2015), 34.

12. Gillian Youngs, *Global Political Economy in the Information Age: Power and Inequality* (New York: Routledge, 2007), 86.

13. Kirby Reiling and Cynthia Brady, *Climate Change and Conflict* (Washington, DC: United States Agency for International Development, 2015).

14. Charles E. Merriam, *Political Power: Its Composition and Incidence* (New York: McGraw-Hill, 1934), 325–326. While reviewing this book, C. J. Friedrich observed that Merriam was one of those American political scientists whose "pride is their realism": Carl Joachim Friedrich, "Review of 'Political Power' by Charles Merriam," *Harvard Law Review* 48, no. 5 (1935): 876–879, 876.

15. York Willbern, "Is the New Public Administration Still with Us?," review of *Toward a New Public Administration: The Minnowbrook Perspective* by Frank Marini, *Public Administration in a Time of Turbulence* by Dwight Waldo, *Organizational Frontiers and Human Values* by Warren H. Schmidt, and *The Administrative Revolution: Notes on the Passing of Organization Man* by George E. Berkley, *Public Administration Review* 33, no. 4 (1973): 373–378, 373–374.

16. Donald Kettl, *Escaping Jurassic Government* (Washington, DC: Brookings Institution, 2016), 2 and 171.

17. Ibid., 1.

12. Time and Progress

1. For example, see Hyman P. Minsky, *Stabilizing an Unstable Economy* (New Haven, CT: Yale University Press, 2008).

2. Hendrik Spruyt, *Global Horizons: An Introduction to International Relations* (Toronto: University of Toronto Press, 2009), 18.

3. Jo Guldi and David Armitage, *The History Manifesto* (Cambridge: Cambridge University Press, 2014), 7.

4. Karen Orren and Stephen Skowronek, *The Search for American Political Development* (New York: Cambridge University Press, 2004), 1. The shorthand way of expressing this position is that "history matters": Sven Steinmo, "Historical Institutionalism," in *Approaches and Methodologies in the Social Sciences*, ed. Donatella Della Porta and Michael Keating (Cambridge: Cambridge University Press, 2008), 118–138, 127.

5. Alasdair Roberts, *Four Crises of American Democracy: Representation, Mastery, Discipline, Anticipation* (New York: Oxford University Press, 2017), 181–182.

6. Karl L. Trever, "Administrative History in Federal Archives," *American Archivist* 4, no. 3 (1941): 159–169, 7; See also Roy F. Nichols, "Administrative History," *Public Administration Review* 4, no. 3 (1944): 240–241.

7. Lynton K. Caldwell, "The Relevance of Administrative History," *International Review of Administrative Sciences* 21, no. 3 (1955): 453–461.

8. Guy B. Adams, "Enthralled with Modernity: The Historical Context of Knowledge and Theory Development in Public Administration," *Public Administration Review* 52, no. 4 (1992): 363–373; Hindy Lauer Schachter, "History and Identity in the Field of Public Administration," *Administrative Theory and Praxis* 20, no. 1 (1998): 16–22, 16; Larry S. Luton, "History and American Public Administration," *Administration and Society* 31, no. 2 (1999): 205–221; Robert F. Durant, "Taking Time Seriously: Progressivism, the Business–Social Science Nexus, and the Paradox of American Administrative Reform," *PS: Political Science and Politics* 47, no. 1 (2014): 8–18, 14–15; and Robert F. Durant and David Rosenbloom, "The Hollowing of American Public Administration," *American Review of Public Administration* 47, no. 7 (2016): 9–10.

9. Christopher Pollitt, *Time, Policy, Management: Governing with the Past* (New York: Oxford University Press, 2008), 29.

10. Jos C. N. Raadschelders, "Is American Public Administration Detached from Historical Context?," *American Review of Public Administration* 40, no. 3 (2010): 235 and 241.

11. Peter Miller, "The Dangers of Retrospective Myopia," *Journal of Portfolio Management* 6, no. 1 (1979): 67–73.

12. This phrase was coined by Richard Neustadt and Ernest May: Richard E. Neustadt and Ernest R. May, *Thinking in Time* (New York: Free Press, 1986), xiii.

13. Arthur M. Schlesinger, *The Cycles of American History* (Boston: Houghton Mifflin, 1986), 30–31.

14. Andrew Healy and Neil Malhotra, "Retrospective Voting Reconsidered," *Annual Review of Political Science* 16, no. 1 (2013): 285–306; Larry M. Bartels, *Unequal Democracy: The Political Economy of the New Gilded Age* (Princeton, NJ: Princeton University Press, 2008), chap. 4.

15. The same point is made by Joseph Nye: Joseph S. Nye, *Is the American Century Over?* (Cambridge: Polity, 2015), chap. 2.

16. For discussion of the concept of progress, see: J. B. Bury, *The Idea of Progress: An Inquiry into Its Origin and Growth* (New York: Dover, 1987); Robert A. Nisbet, *History of the Idea of Progress* (New Brunswick, NJ: Transaction, 1994).

17. See the discussion of Plato, Polybius, and Machiavelli in Alan Ryan, *On Politics* (New York: Norton, 2012), 68, 123–127, 383.

18. See Beard's introduction to Bury, *Idea of Progress*.

19. Michael E. Latham, *The Right Kind of Revolution: Modernization, Development, and U.S. Foreign Policy from the Cold War to the Present* (Ithaca, NY: Cornell University Press, 2011), 3.

20. James Reston, "The Crisis of Democracy," *New York Times*, March 3, 1974.

21. Munich Security Conference, *Munich Security Report 2017: Post-Truth, Post-West, Post-Order?* (Munich: Munich Security Conference, 2017), 5.

22. Herbert Butterfield, *The Whig Interpretation of History* (London: G. Bell and Sons, 1931), 23.

23. I elaborate on this idea in two books: Roberts, *Four Crises of American Democracy*, and Roberts, *Can Government Do Anything Right?* (Cambridge: Polity, 2018).

13. Unexceptionalism

1. Ira Katznelson and Martin Shefter, *Shaped by War and Trade: International Influences on American Political Development* (Princeton, NJ: Princeton University Press, 2002), 14.

2. John Gerring, "APD from a Methodological Point of View," *Studies in American Political Development* 17, no. 1 (2003): 82–102, 84.

3. "Great anomaly": Stephen Skowronek, *Building a New American State* (New York: Cambridge University Press, 1982), 6. "Distinctly American phenomena": Brian Balogh, *A Government out of Sight: The Mystery of National Authority in Nineteenth-Century America* (New York: Cambridge University Press, 2009), 19–20.

4. Germany and Italy were unified in the late nineteenth century. The current French system of government is known as the Fifth Republic. The state known as the United Kingdom of Great Britain and Ireland was established in 1800.

5. Roberto Stefan Foa and Anna Nemirovskaya, "How State Capacity Varies within Frontier States: A Multicountry Subnational Analysis," *Governance* 29, no. 3 (2016): 411–432.

6. Derick W. Brinkerhoff, "Introduction," in *Governance in Post-Conflict Societies*, ed. Derick W. Brinkerhoff (New York: Routledge, 2007), 17.

7. Particularly in the 1990s, when policy regarding state reform in the developing world was shaped by the "Washington consensus."

8. "Liberal absolutism" is the phrase used by Louis Hartz: Louis Hartz, *The Liberal Tradition in America* (San Diego, CA: Harcourt Brace Jovanovich, 1991).

9. Or Rosenboim, *The Emergence of Globalism: Visions of World Order in Britain and the United States, 1939–1950* (Princeton, NJ: Princeton University Press, 2017), 110–111.

10. Bobo Lo, *Russia and the New World Disorder* (Washington, DC: Brookings Institution Press, 2015), 10–17.

11. Wei-Wei Zhang, *The China Wave: Rise of a Civilizational State* (Hackensack, NJ: World Century, 2012), 156.

12. Aga Khan, *India in Transition: A Study in Political Evolution* (Bombay: Bennett, 1918), 1; Central Intelligence Agency, *Country Profile: India* (Washington, DC: Central Intelligence Agency, 1973), 1.

13. Aparna Pande, *From Chanakya to Modi: The Evolution of India's Foreign Policy* (Noida, India: HarperCollins India, 2017), chap. 1.

14. Matt Andrews, "Good Government Means Different Things in Different Countries," *Governance* 23, no. 1 (2010): 7–35.

14. Efficiency or Extravagance

1. Albert Gore, *Creating a Government That Works Better and Costs Less* (New York: Times, 1993), i; Tony Bovaird and Elke Loeffler, *Public Management and Governance*, 3rd ed. (London: Routledge, 2016), 5.

2. Laurence E. Lynn Jr., *Public Management: Thinking and Acting in Three Dimensions*, 2nd ed. (Los Angeles: Sage, 2016), 104.

3. Henry Bruère et al., "Efficiency in City Government," *Annals of the American Academy of Political and Social Science* 41 (1912): 3–22.

4. Jonathan Monten and Andrew Bennett, "Models of Crisis Decision Making and the 1990–91 Gulf War," *Security Studies* 19, no. 3 (2010): 486–520, 503.

5. Alain C. Enthoven and K. Wayne Smith, *How Much Is Enough? Shaping the Defense Program, 1961–1969* (New York: Harper & Row, 1971), 331–332. Powell called Vietnam a "half-hearted half-war": Colin L. Powell, *My American Journey* (New York: Random House, 1995), 143.

6. Harlan Ullman, James P. Wade, and L. A. Edney, *Shock and Awe: Achieving Rapid Dominance* (Washington, DC: NDU Press, 1996), 16.

7. Conrad Crane, "Fighting Insurgencies and Terrorists in Post-Conflict Situations," in *International Statebuilding and Reconstruction Efforts*, ed. Joachim Krause and Charles K. Mallory (Farmington Hills, MI: Barbara Budrich, 2010), 99–116, 108.

8. Thomas P. Slaughter, *The Whiskey Rebellion: Frontier Epilogue to the American Revolution* (New York: Oxford University Press, 1986), 198.

9. Eugene Leach, "The Literature of Riot Duty," *Radical History Review* 53 (1993): 23–50, 43.

10. Henry Adams Bellows, *A Treatise on Riot Duty for the National Guard* (Washington: Government Printing Office, 1920), 97.

11. Alex Vitale, "The Command and Control and Miami Models at the 2004 Republican National Convention: New Forms of Policing Protest," *Mobilization* 12, no. 4 (2007): 403–415, 405–408.

12. Richard Winton, "How Would the LAPD Handle a Riot Today?," *Los Angeles Times*, April 27, 2017.

13. Jan Morris, *Heaven's Command: An Imperial Progress* (New York, Harcourt Brace Jovanovich, 1980), 271.

14. Deyan Sudjic, *The Edifice Complex: How the Rich and Powerful Shape the World* (New York: Penguin, 2005), 3 and 10.

15. Lois A. Craig, *The Federal Presence: Architecture, Politics, and Symbols in United States Government Building* (Cambridge, MA: MIT Press, 1978), 150.

16. "A Visit to the Nation's Capital," *Highland Weekly News* (Hillsborough, Ohio), February 17, 1881, 2.

17. Generally, see Joseph Maresca, *WPA Buildings, Architecture and Art of the New Deal* (Atglen, PA: Schiffer, 2017).

18. Richard R. John, *Spreading the News: The American Postal System from Franklin to Morse* (Cambridge, MA: Harvard University Press, 1995), 10; Winifred Gallagher, *How the Post Office Created America* (New York: Penguin Random House, 2016), 2–3 and 105.

19. Suzanne Mettler, *The Submerged State: How Invisible Government Policies Undermine American Democracy* (Chicago: University of Chicago Press, 2011), 5. See also Donald F. Kettl, *The Next Government of the United States* (New York: W. W. Norton & Co., 2009), chap. 2, and Donald Kettl, *Escaping Jurassic Government* (Washington, DC: Brookings Institution, 2016), chap. 4.

20. Martin Landau advanced a different argument against leanness, praising the virtues of redundancy: "Redundancy, Rationality, and the Problem of Duplication and Overlap," *Public Administration Review* 29.4 (1969): 346–358.

15. Tight or Loose Control

1. Peter H. Schuck, *Why Government Fails So Often* (Princeton, NJ: Princeton University Press, 2014), chap. 9.

2. Alasdair Roberts, "The Nation-State: Not Dead Yet," *Wilson Quarterly* Summer 2015, 8.

3. Kenichi Ohmae, *The End of the Nation State: The Rise of Regional Economies* (New York: Free Press, 1995), 214–215.
4. Freedom House website at https://freedomhouse.org.
5. Fraser Institute website at https://www.fraserinstitute.org.
6. Jonathan Rodden, "Comparative Federalism and Decentralization: On Meaning and Measurement," *Comparative Politics* 36, no. 4 (2004): 481–500; Maksym Ivanyna and Anwar Shah, *How Close Is Your Government to Its People?*, WPS6138 (Washington, DC: World Bank, 2012), 19–25.
7. Generally, see Lynn Hunt, *Inventing Human Rights: A History* (New York: W. W. Norton & Co., 2007); Samuel Moyn, *The Last Utopia: Human Rights in History* (Cambridge, MA: Belknap, 2010).
8. *New State Ice Co. v. Liebmann*, 285 U.S. 262 (1932), at 306.
9. William R. Allen, "Economics, Economists, and Economic Policy: Modern American Experiences," *History of Political Economy* 9, no. 1 (1977): 48–88.

16. Separation or Connection

1. In his farewell address of 1796, Washington said that the United States should not "entangle our peace and prosperity" in European conflicts. Five years later, in his first inaugural address, Thomas Jefferson promised "honest friendship with all nations, entangling alliances with none."
2. Alexis de Tocqueville, *Democracy in America* (New York: Penguin, 2003), 99.
3. Senator Joseph Underwood of Kentucky, in the *Congressional Globe*, December 3, 1851, 26.
4. James Bryce, *The American Commonwealth* (New York: Macmillan, 1914), 1:68 and 3:117.
5. Paul M. Kennedy, *The Rise and Fall of the Great Powers: Economic Change and Military Conflict from 1500 to 2000* (New York: Vintage, 1987), 187.
6. Alasdair Roberts, *America's First Great Depression: Economic Crisis and Political Disorder after the Panic of 1837* (Ithaca, NY: Cornell University Press, 2012), figs. 1 and 2.
7. Michael Mandelbaum, *The Case for Goliath: How America Acts as the World's Government in the 21st Century* (New York: Public Affairs, 2005), chap. 1.
8. Generally see Ken'ichi Ōmae, *The Borderless World: Power and Strategy in the Interlinked Economy* (New York: HarperBusiness, 1990).
9. Louis Dow Scisco, "Political Nativism in New York State" (PhD diss., Columbia University, 1901), 16.
10. Samuel P. Huntington, "Dead Souls: The Denationalization of the American Elite," *National Interest*, no. 75 (2004): 5–18, 5–6.
11. Matt Clinch, "The 'Party of Davos' Wakes up to the New, New World Order," *CNBC*, January 9, 2017.
12. Michael Ignatieff, *The Ordinary Virtues: Moral Order in a Divided World* (Cambridge, MA: Harvard University Press, 2017), 23.

17. Present or Future

1. Ronald Wright, *A Short History of Progress* (Edinburgh: Canongate, 2004), 108 and 131.
2. Department of Defense, *Quadrennial Defense Review* (Washington, DC: Department of Defense, 2014), 8.
3. Generally see Jonathan Boston, *Governing for the Future: Designing Democratic Institutions for a Better Tomorrow* (Bingley, UK: Emerald, 2016).
4. Oxford Martin Commission for Future Generations, *Now for the Long Term* (Oxford: Oxford Martin Commission for Future Generations, October 2013), 47.
5. Dublin University Magazine, "A Few Words on the Crisis," *Dublin University Magazine* 17, no. 102 (1841): 777–780, 778–779.
6. Alasdair Roberts, *Four Crises of American Democracy: Representation, Mastery, Discipline, Anticipation* (New York: Oxford University Press, 2017), 147–149.
7. Thomas Jefferson, *Memoir, Correspondence, and Miscellanies from the Papers of Thomas Jefferson* (Charlottesville, VA: F. Carr, 1829), 30.
8. Jeremy L. Caradonna, *Sustainability: A History* (New York: Oxford University Press, 2016), 29.
9. Michèle B. Bättig and Thomas Bernauer, "National Institutions and Global Public Goods: Are Democracies More Cooperative in Climate Change Policy?," *International Organization* 63, no. 2 (2009): 281–308.

18. Commitment or Equivocation

1. Generally see Douglass C. North and Barry R. Weingast, "Constitutions and Commitment: The Evolution of Institutions Governing Public Choice in Seventeenth-Century England," *Journal of Economic History* 49, no. 4 (1989): 803–832; Stephen H. Haber, Armando Razo, and Noel Maurer, *The Politics of Property Rights: Political Instability, Credible Commitments, and Economic Growth in Mexico, 1876–1929* (Cambridge: Cambridge University Press, 2003).
2. Generally see Sylvia Maxfield, *Gatekeepers of Growth: The International Political Economy of Central Banking in Developing Countries* (Princeton, NJ: Princeton University Press, 1997).
3. Brian Levy and Pablo T. Spiller, "The Institutional Foundations of Regulatory Commitment: A Comparative Analysis of Telecommunications Regulation," *Journal of Law, Economics and Organization* 10, no. 2 (1994): 201–246.
4. Generally see David M. Primo, *Rules and Restraint: Government Spending and the Design of Institutions* (Chicago: University of Chicago Press, 2007).
5. Thomas L. Friedman, *The Lexus and the Olive Tree: Understanding Globalization* (New York: Farrar, Straus & Giroux, 1999), 184.
6. Barbara F. Walter, "The Critical Barrier to Civil War Settlement," *International Organization* 51, no. 3 (1997): 335–364; James Fearon, "Commitment Problems and the Spread of Ethnic Conflict," in *The International Spread of Ethnic Conflict*, ed. David Lake and Donald Rothchild (Princeton, NJ: Princeton University Press, 1998), 107–126.

7. Generally see David C. Hendrickson, *Peace Pact: The Lost World of the American Founding*, American Political Thought (Lawrence: University Press of Kansas, 2003).
8. Margaret Levi, "A State of Trust," in *Trust and Governance*, ed. A. Braithwaite and M. Levi (New York: Russell Sage, 1998), 77–101.
9. Thomas Edward Flores and Irfan Nooruddin, "The Effect of Elections on Post-conflict Peace and Reconstruction," *Journal of Politics* 74, no. 2 (2012): 558–570.
10. Alexis de Tocqueville, *Democracy in America* (New York: Penguin, 2003), 1:98.
11. On path dependence, see generally Paul Pierson, *Politics in Time* (Princeton, NJ: Princeton University Press, 2004). On sclerosis: Mancur Olson, *The Rise and Decline of Nations* (New Haven, CT: Yale University Press, 1982).
12. I am not suggesting that they ought to.

19. Planning or Improvisation

1. Charles E. Merriam, "The Possibilities of Planning," *American Journal of Sociology* 49, no. 5 (1944): 397–407, 397.
2. The board was dismantled in 1943, when conservatives in Congress refused to authorize continued funding.
3. Lippmann, *Drift and Mastery* (New York: Mitchell Kennerley, 1914), 269.
4. "The experience of our day shows that no system, political or economic, unless it faces frankly the grave realities of modern economic and governmental life and boldly takes the initiative in broad plans for a better day, can be protected against explosion that wrecks and twists" the social order: National Planning Board, *Final Report: A Plan for Planning* (Washington, DC: National Planning Board, 1934), 22.
5. Franklin D. Roosevelt, *Looking Forward* (New York: John Day, 1933), 13.
6. Walter Duranty, *USSR: The Story of Soviet Russia* (London: H. Hamilton, 1944), 153.
7. Herbert W. Schneider, *Making the Fascist State* (New York: Oxford University Press, 1928), 113; John P. Diggins, "Flirtation with Fascism: American Pragmatic Liberals and Mussolini's Italy," *American Historical Review* 71, no. 2 (1966): 487–506, 493.
8. Hans Speier, "Class Structure and 'Total War,'" *American Sociological Review* 4, no. 3 (1939): 370–380, 371. The term was coined by General Erich Ludendorff: see Erich Ludendorff, *Der Totale Krieg* (Munich: Ludendorffs Verlag, 1935).
9. William James, *Memories and Studies* (London: Longmans, Green, 1911), 287–288.
10. Alfred J. Kahn, "What Is Social Planning?," in *Theory and Practice of Social Planning*, ed. Alfred J. Kahn (New York: Russell Sage Foundation, 1969), 1–27, 13.
11. Alfred J. Kahn, "The Framework in Perspective," in Kahn, *Theory and Practice of Social Planning*, 328–340, 328.
12. More recently, Martin Wolf has observed: "The analysis of fundamental macro-economic theory suggests substantial ignorance of how our economies work. . . . We may never understand how such complex systems . . . actually function": Martin Wolf, "Economics Failed us before the Financial Crisis," *Financial Times*, March 20, 2018.
13. For example, Hans J. Morgenthau, "The Limitations of Science and the Problem of Social Planning," *Ethics* 54, no. 3 (1944): 174–185.

14. Robert Fishman et al., "Recreating the Small Town," *Wilson Quarterly* 16, no. 2 (1992): 136–141, 137. An early warning about unintended consequences was provided by the Scottish philosopher Adam Ferguson. "The most refined politicians," Ferguson warned in 1767, "do not know whither they are leading the state by their projects": Adam Ferguson, *An Essay on the History of Civil Society*, 8th ed. (Philadelphia: A. Finley, 1819), 222–228.

15. Roosevelt, *Looking Forward*, 51.

16. Kuno Francke, William Guild Howard, and Isidore Singer, *The German Classics of the Nineteenth and Twentieth Centuries*, vol. 10 (Albany: J. B. Lyon, 1913), 288.

20. Research

1. For example, see David J. Schnall, "Lack of Rigor," *Public Administration Review* 41, no. 3 (1981): 403–404; Howard E. McCurdy and Robert E. Cleary, "Why Can't We Resolve the Research Issue in Public Administration?," *Public Administration Review* 44, no. 1 (1984): 49–55; James L. Perry and Kenneth L. Kraemer, "Research Methodology in the Public Administration Review, 1975–1984," *Public Administration Review* 46, no. 3 (1986): 215–226; Robert A. Stallings and James M. Ferris, "Public Administration Research: Work in PAR, 1940–1984," *Public Administration Review* 48, no. 1 (1988): 580–587; David J. Houston and Sybil M. Delevan, "Public Administration Research: An Assessment of Journal Publications," *Public Administration Review* 50, no. 6 (1990): 674–681; and Laurence E. Lynn Jr., "Public Management Research: The Triumph of Art over Science," *Journal of Policy Analysis and Management* 13, no. 2 (1994): 231–259.

2. John W. Ellwood, "Challenges to Public Policy and Public Management Education," *Journal of Policy Analysis and Management* 27, no. 1 (2008): 172–187, 174.

3. Richard F. Elmore, "Graduate Education in Public Management: Working the Seams of Government," *Journal of Policy Analysis and Management* 6, no. 1 (1986): 70; Steven Kelman, *Public Administration and Organization Studies* (Cambridge, MA: Kennedy School of Government, 2007), 4.

4. Eric Welch and Wilson Wong, "Public Administration in a Global Context: Bridging the Gaps of Theory and Practice between Western and Non-Western Nations," *Public Administration Review* 58, no. 1 (1998): 40–49, 44.

5. David W. Pitts and Sergio Fernandez, "The State of Public Management Research: An Analysis of Scope and Methodology," *International Public Management Journal* 12, no. 4 (2009): 399–420, 405 and 411; Jos C. N. Raadschelders and Kwang-Hoon Lee, "Trends in the Study of Public Administration: Empirical and Qualitative Observations from Public Administration Review, 2000–2009," *Public Administration Review* 71, no. 1 (2011): 24 and 27. See also Richard C. Box, "An Examination of the Debate over Research in Public Administration," *Public Administration Review* 52, no. 1 (1992): 62–69, 63.

6. H. George Frederickson et al., *The Public Administration Theory Primer*, 2nd ed. (Boulder, CO: Westview, 2012), 3–4.

7. Steven Kelman, "If You Want to Be a Good Fill-in-the-Blank Manager, Be a Good Plain-Vanilla Manager," *PS: Political Science and Politics* 44, no. 2 (2011): 241–246, 244.

8. It could be argued that some of the most important contributions of public management scholarship have come in the form of concepts or frameworks that are useful in structuring conversations about important questions; for example, the alternative frameworks for understanding decision-making proposed by Graham T. Allison and Philip Zelikow or the framework for thinking about organizational strategy proposed by Mark Moore: Graham T. Allison and Philip Zelikow, *Essence of Decision: Explaining the Cuban Missile Crisis* (New York: Longman, 1999); Mark Moore, *Creating Public Value: Strategic Management in Government* (Cambridge, MA: Harvard University Press, 1995). Both of these frameworks were invented before the push for rigor in public management research intensified in the 1980s.

9. Richard M. Walker, Oliver James, and Gene A. Brewer, "Replication, Experiments and Knowledge in Public Management Research," *Public Management Review* 19, no. 9 (2017): 1221–1234. "There is an urgent need for replication studies": Richard M. Walker, M. Jin Lee, and Oliver James, "Replication of Experimental Research: Implications for the Study of Public Management," in *Experiments in Public Management Research*, ed. Oliver James, Sebastian Jilke, and Gregg Van Ryzin (Cambridge: Cambridge University Press, 2017), 439–460, 457. See also Mogens Jin Pedersen and Justin M. Stritch, "RNICE Model: Evaluating the Contribution of Replication Studies in Public Administration and Management Research," *Public Administration Review*, forthcoming.

10. A range of "contextual factors" are discussed in the introduction to Kenneth J. Meier, Amanda Rutherford and Claudia N. Avellaneda, *Comparative Public Management: Why National, Environmental, and Organizational Context Matters* (Washington, DC, Georgetown University Press, 2017). Similarly, see Gary Johns, "Reflections on the 2016 Decade Award: Incorporating Context in Organizational Research," *Academy of Management Review* 42, no. 4 (2017): 577–595, and Jay J. Van Bavel, et al., "Contextual Sensitivity in Scientific Reproducibility," *Proceedings of the National Academy of Sciences* 113, no. 23 (2016): 6454–6459.

11. For discussion about the abstraction and "slipperiness" of many concepts used in public management scholarship, see Christopher Pollitt and Peter Hupe, "Talking about Government," *Public Management Review* 13, no. 5 (2011): 641–658.

12. Generally see James Mahoney and Dietrich Rueschemeyer, *Comparative Historical Analysis in the Social Sciences* (New York: Cambridge University Press, 2003); Matthew Lange, *Comparative-Historical Methods* (Los Angeles: Sage, 2013); James Mahoney and Kathleen Ann Thelen, *Advances in Comparative-Historical Analysis* (New York: Cambridge University Press, 2015).

13. Rogan Kersh, "The Growth of American Political Development: The View from the Classroom," *Perspectives on Politics* 3, no. 2 (2005): 335–345, 335. The subfield has its own journal, *Studies in American Political Development*, which began in 1986. There is now a "shared core" of "canonic works" in APD that are taught in graduate programs across the United States: ibid., 344; Karen Orren and Stephen Skowronek, *The Search for American Political Development* (New York: Cambridge University Press, 2004), 3 and 35. The subfield is supported by the politics and history section of the American Political Science Association, which by 2010 had more than six hundred members—considerably more than the APSA's public administration section: Michael

Brintnall, "Executive Director's Report," *PS: Political Science and Politics* 43, no. 1 (2010): 172–180, 180.

14. Robert F. Durant, "Taking Time Seriously: Progressivism, the Business–Social Science Nexus, and the Paradox of American Administrative Reform," *PS: Political Science and Politics* 47, no. 1 (2014): 10; Robert F. Durant and David Rosenbloom, "The Hollowing of American Public Administration," *American Review of Public Administration* 47, no. 7 (2016): 20; H. Briton Milward, et al., "Is Public Management Neglecting the State?" Governance 29, no. 3 (2016): 311–334, 330; Christopher Pollitt, "Public Administration Research since 1980: Slipping Away from the Real World," *International Journal of Public Sector Management* (2017): 7–8.

21. Teaching

1. According to the Council of Graduate Schools, 83,000 people were enrolled in graduate programs in "public administration and services" in 2016; however, this includes programs in social work: Council of Graduate Schools, *Graduate Enrollment and Degrees: 2006 to 2016* (Washington, DC: Council of Graduate Schools, 2016), Table B.13. The National Center for Education Statistics reports that 47,000 people received graduate degrees in public administration and social services in 2015–2016: https://nces.ed.gov/programs/digest/d17/tables/dt17_323.10.asp. The Network of Schools of Public Policy, Affairs, and Administration (NASPAA) reported that there were 20,358 students in accredited graduate programs in 2016-2017: https://accreditation.naspaa.org/resources/data-on-accredited-programs/. Many more students are completing undergraduate programs with a major in public administration or public affairs.

2. I refer to graduate programs that are highly ranked according to the survey conducted by *US News and World Report*.

3. Mark Moore, *Creating Public Value: Strategic Management in Government* (Cambridge, MA: Harvard University Press, 1995), 73.

4. "The exponents and interpreters of public administration accepted the Great Society.... They believed in the program of the welfare state": Arthur W. Macmahon, review of *The Administrative State* by Dwight Waldo and of *Freedom and the Administrative State* by Joseph Goldfarb, *Public Administration Review* 8, no. 3 (1948): 203–211, 204. See also Charles E. Merriam, "The Ends of Government," *American Political Science Review* 38, no. 1 (1944): 30–34.

5. Top-ranked institutions that have such a requirement include the Maxwell School of Syracuse University, the University of Southern California, and the University of Georgia.

6. A U.S.-centric approach was recommended by the ASPA Task Force on Educating for Excellence in the master of public administration degree: Nicholas Henry et al., "Understanding Excellence in Public Administration: The Report of the Task Force on Educating for Excellence in the Master of Public Administration Degree of the American Society for Public Administration," *Journal of Public Affairs Education* 15, no. 2 (2009): 117–133, 122–123.

7. Kedar Pavgi, "The Best International Relations Master's Programs," *Foreign Policy*, January 3, 2012, 1–11.

8. Course description, SA.100.761, Theories of International Relations, https://www.sais-jhu.edu/graduate-studies/courses/theories-international-relations.

9. Course description, MSFS 510, International Relations: Theory and Practice, https://myaccess.georgetown.edu/pls/bninbp/bwckctlg.p_disp_course_detail?cat_term_in=201730&subj_code_in=MSFS&crse_numb_in=510.

10. Course description, INAF U6804, Conceptual Foundations of International Politics, http://bulletin.columbia.edu/sipa/programs/mia/#requirementstext.

11. Carmen Mezzera, "Keeping Ahead in Uncertain Times," *Foreign Affairs* 96, no. 5 (2017), Supplement 1–3, 1.

12. The same holds true for undergraduate programs. Robert Vitalis observes, "Every year thousands of undergraduates across the United States sign up for a class titled 'Introduction to International Relations'... [and] learn that three broad rival theoretical traditions vie for explanatory primacy among specialists": Robert Vitalis, *White World Order, Black Power Politics: The Birth of American International Relations* (Ithaca, NY: Cornell University Press, 2015), 5.

22. Practice

1. Francis Fukuyama, "America: The Failed State," *Prospect*, December 13, 2017; David J. Rothkopf, "Is American a Failing State?," *Foreign Policy*, May 10, 2017.

2. Reuters, "Chinese State Media: U.S. Government Shutdown Exposes 'Chronic Flaws,'" *Reuters News Service*, January 20, 2018.

3. Alasdair Roberts, "Bridging Levels of Public Administration: How Macro Shapes Meso and Micro," Working paper, March 2019. https://papers.ssrn.com/sol3/papers.cfm?abstract_id=3291763.

4. "Policymakers customarily work within a framework of ideas and standards that specifies not only the goals of policy and the kinds of instruments that can be used to attain them, but also the very nature of the problems they are meant to be addressing": Peter Hall, "Policy Paradigms, Social Learning, and the State: The Case of Economic Policymaking in Britain," *Comparative Politics* 25, no. 3 (1993): 275–296, 279. Similarly: "The deliberation of public policy takes place within a realm of discourse... policies are made within some system of ideas and standards which is comprehensible and plausible to the actors involved": Charles W. Anderson, "The Logic of Public Problems," in *Comparing Public Policies*, ed. Douglas Ashford (Beverly Hills, CA: Sage, 1978), 19–41, 23.

5. Anthony Cheung, "The Politics of New Public Management: Some Experience from Reforms in East Asia," in *New Public Management: Current Trends and Future Prospects*, ed. Kate McLaughlin, Stephen Osborne, and Ewan Ferlie (London: Routledge, 2002), 245.

6. Woodrow Wilson, "The Study of Administration," *Political Science Quarterly* 2, no. 2 (1887): 201.

7. Louis Brownlow, "Woodrow Wilson and Public Administration," *Public Administration Review* 16, no. 2 (1956): 77–81, 81.

Conclusion

1. National Academy of Public Administration, "About Us," accessed December 7, 2018, https://www.napawash.org/about-us/who-we-are/.
2. National Academy of Public Administration, "Grand Challenges in Public Administration," accessed December 7, 2018, https://www.napawash.org/grand-challenges-in-public-administration/.
3. "What we've got here is a relatively new but quite powerful working consensus between the political parties on most major issues": Nicholas Lemann, "The New American Consensus," *New York Times*, November 1, 1998.
4. Averages of responses for polls taken between 1997–2003 and 2008–2018: Gallup, "Satisfaction with the United States," accessed December 7, 2018, https://news.gallup.com/poll/1669/general-mood-country.aspx.
5. See Alasdair Roberts, *Four Crises of American Democracy: Representation, Mastery, Discipline, Anticipation* (New York: Oxford University Press, 2017).
6. "The two major political parties agree on fundamentals; they offer alternative policies to the voters only on relatively small points of difference": Charles Lindblom, "The Science of 'Muddling Through'" *Public Administration Review* 19 no. 2 (1959): 79–88, 84.
7. In its quadrennial review of policy, the Department of Defense considers the next twenty years. The State Department plans for the "next generation of American diplomacy." The Congressional Budget Office's "long-term outlook" is thirty years. Trustees of the Social Security and Medicare programs look seventy-five years into the future.
8. Walter Lippmann, *Drift and Mastery* (New York: Mitchell Kennerley, 1914), 160.
9. Speech at the Bálványos Free Summer University and Youth Camp, July 26, 2014.
10. Arch Puddington, *Breaking Down Democracy: Goals, Strategies, and Methods of Modern Authoritarians* (Washington, DC: Freedom House, 2017), chap. 5.
11. Wei-Wei Zhang, *The China Wave* (Hackensack, NJ: World Century, 2012), chap. 6.2.

A Glossary of States

1. Harvey C. Mansfield, "Government," *American Journal of Sociology* 47, no. 6 (1942): 958–970; Joseph Rosenfarb, *Freedom and the Administrative State* (New York: Harper, 1948).
2. James Burnham, *The Managerial Revolution* (New York: John Day, 1941), 71–72.
3. John Kenneth Galbraith, *The New Industrial State* (Boston: Houghton Mifflin, 1967), 73-88.

4. Joan C. Henderson, "Planning for Success: Singapore, the Model City-State?," *Journal of International Affairs* 65, no. 2 (2012): 69–83; Rachel Morris, "Modern City State," *AQ: Australian Quarterly* 83, no. 2 (2012): 26–28.

5. David Stasavage, *States of Credit: Size, Power, and the Development of European Polities* (Princeton, NJ: Princeton University Press, 2011), chap. 1.

6. Generally, see M. I. Finley, *Politics in the Ancient World* (Cambridge: Cambridge University Press, 1983).

7. James J. Sheehan, *The Monopoly of Violence: Why Europeans Hate Going to War* (London: Faber & Faber, 2008), xx and 172–173.

8. With regard to China: Martin Jacques, "Understanding China," *Los Angeles Times*, November 22, 2009; Wei-Wei Zhang, *The China Wave: Rise of a Civilizational State* (Hackensack, NJ: World Century, 2012), chap. 3. With regard to India: Martin R. Doornbos and Sudipta Kaviraj, *Dynamics of State Formation: India and Europe Compared* (Thousand Oaks, CA: Sage, 1997), chap. 15; Ravinder Kumar, "India: A 'Nation-State' or 'Civilisation-State'?," *South Asia: Journal of South Asian Studies* 25, no. 2 (2002): 13–32.

9. Mehtap Söyler, *The Turkish Deep State: State Consolidation, Civil-Military Relations and Democracy* (Florence, Italy: Taylor & Francis, 2015).

10. Ryan Gingeras, "In the Hunt for the 'Sultans of Smack': Dope, Gangsters and the Construction of the Turkish Deep State," *Middle East Journal* 65, no. 3 (2011): 426–441, 439.

11. Lofgren, *The Deep State: The Fall of the Constitution and the Rise of a Shadow Government* (New York: Viking, 2016), 5.

12. For a recent review of the concept, see Stephen Haggard, *Developmental States* (Cambridge, UK, Cambridge University Press, 2018).

13. David M. Trubek, "Toward a Social Theory of Law: An Essay on the Study of Law and Development," *Yale Law Journal* 82, no. 1 (1972): 1–50, 36–37.

14. Generally, see: Chalmers Johnson, *MITI and the Japanese Miracle: The Growth of Industrial Policy, 1925–1975* (Stanford, CA: Stanford University Press, 1982).

15. Michael W. Doyle, *Empires: Cornell Studies in Comparative History* (Ithaca, NY: Cornell University Press, 1986), 45; Krishan Kumar, *Visions of Empire: How Five Imperial Regimes Shaped the World* (Princeton, NJ: Princeton University Press, 2017), 16.

16. Kumar, *Visions of Empire*, 15.

17. For one defense of the imperial model, see: Alpheus Henry Snow, *The Administration of Dependencies: A Study of the Evolution of the Federal Empire* (New York: G. P. Putnam's Sons, 1902).

18. Michael Hardt and Antonio Negri, *Empire* (Cambridge, MA: Harvard University Press, 2000), xi–xii.

19. For discussions of this concept, see: John Brewer, *The Sinews of Power: War, Money, and the English State, 1688–1783* (Cambridge, MA: Harvard University Press, 1990); Philip Harling and Peter Mandler, "From 'Fiscal-Military' State to Laissez-Faire State, 1760–1850," *Journal of British Studies* 32, no. 1 (1993): 44–70; Christopher Storrs, ed., *The Fiscal Military State in Eighteenth-Century Europe* (Burlington, VT: Ashgate, 2008).

20. Gerald B. Helman and Steven R. Ratner, "Saving Failed States," *Foreign Policy*, no. 89 (1992): 3–20.

21. Thomas Risse, *Governance without a State? Policies and Politics in Areas of Limited Statehood* (New York: Columbia University Press, 2011), 4.

22. Benjamin Miller, "Between the Revisionist and the Frontier State: Regional Variations in State War-Propensity," *Review of International Studies* 35 (2009): 85–119; Roberto Stefan Foa and Anna Nemirovskaya, "How State Capacity Varies within Frontier States: A Multicountry Subnational Analysis," *Governance* 29, no. 3 (2016): 411–432.

23. Frederick Jackson Turner, *The Frontier in American History* (New York: Henry Holt, 1920), 1–2.

24. Harold D. Lasswell, "The Garrison State," *American Journal of Sociology* 46, no. 4 (1941): 455–468; Harold D. Lasswell, "Does the Garrison State Threaten Civil Rights?," *Annals of the American Academy of Political and Social Science* 275 (1951): 111–116. A preliminary formulation was offered in Harold Laswell, "Sino-Japanese Crisis: The Garrison State versus the Civilian State," *China Quarterly* 11 (1937): 455–468.

25. Generally, see: Fred J. Cook, *The Warfare State* (New York: Macmillan, 1962); Fred J. Cook, "The Warfare State," *Annals of the American Academy of Political and Social Science* 351, no. 1 (1964): 102–109; Keith L. Nelson, "The 'Warfare State': History of a Concept," *Pacific Historical Review* 40, no. 2 (1971): 127–143.

26. Generally, see: Leonard S. Rodberg and Derek Shearer, *The Pentagon Watchers: Students Report on the National Security State* (Garden City, NY: Doubleday, 1970); Michael J. Hogan, *A Cross of Iron: Harry S. Truman and the Origins of the National Security State, 1945–1954* (New York: Cambridge University Press, 1998).

27. Generally, see: James Ledbetter, *Unwarranted Influence: Dwight D. Eisenhower and the Military-Industrial Complex* (New Haven, CT: Yale University Press, 2011).

28. H. Brinton Milward and Keith G. Provan, "Governing the Hollow State," *Journal of Public Administration Research and Theory* 10, no. 2 (2000): 359–379.

29. Philip Bobbitt, *The Shield of Achilles* (New York: Knopf, 2002), 228–235.

30. Ferdinand Schevill, "Review of 'Nationalities and National Minorities,'" review of *Nationalities and National Minorities* by Oscar I. Janowsky, *Journal of Modern History* 18, no. 2 (1946): 175–176, 175.

31. Edward Cary Hayes, "Sociological Construction Lines," *American Journal of Sociology* 10, no. 5 (1905): 623–642, 625–626.

32. John Stuart Mill, *Considerations on Representative Government* (London: Parker, Son, & Bourn, 1861), 289.

33. Adrian Hastings, *The Construction of Nationhood: Ethnicity, Religion and Nationalism* (Cambridge, UK: Cambridge University Press, 1997), 3.

34. Aspects of the neoliberal state are discussed by: Stephen Gill, "The Global Panopticon? The Neoliberal State, Economic Life, and Democratic Surveillance," *Alternatives: Global, Local, Political* 20, no. 1 (1995): 1–49; Ian Clark, "Beyond the Great Divide: Globalization and the Theory of International Relations," *Review of International Studies* 24, no. 4 (1998): 479–498, 489–490; Alasdair Roberts, *The Logic of Discipline: Global Capitalism and the New Architecture of Government* (New York: Oxford University Press, 2010).

35. Generally, see: Philip G. Cerny, *The Changing Architecture of Politics: Structure, Agency, and the Future of the State* (London: Sage, 1990); Philipp Genschel and Laura Seelkopf, "The Competition State: The Modern State in a Global Economy," in *Oxford*

Handbook of Transformations of the State, ed. Stephan Leibfried et al. (New York: Oxford University Press, 2015), 237–252.

36. Daniel I. Okimoto, *Between MITI and the Market: Japanese Industrial Policy for High Technology* (Stanford, CA: Stanford University Press, 1989), 152–155, 226.

37. Manuel Castells, *End of Millennium* (Malden, MA: Blackwell, 1998), xxii–xxiii, 383.

38. Manuel Castells, *The Rise of the Network Society* (Malden, MA: Blackwell, 1996), 111; Castells, *End of Millennium*, xxiii, 367. See also Felix Stalder, *Manuel Castells* (Boston: Polity, 2006) and Martin Carnoy and Manuel Castells, "Globalization, the Knowledge Society, and the Network State: Poulantzas at the Millennium," *Global Networks* 1, no. 1 (2001): 1–18.

39. Eduard Bernstein, *Ferdinand Lassalle as a Social Reformer* (London: S. Sonnenschein, 1893), 103–104. See also Wilhelm von Humboldt, *The Sphere and Duties of Government* (London: J. Chapman, 1854).

40. Eduard Meyer and Helene S. White, *England: Its Political Organization and Development and the War against Germany* (Boston: Ritter, 1916), 53.

41. Walter Eucken, *The Foundations of Economics: History and Theory in the Analysis of Economic Reality* (London: W. Hodge, 1950); Wilhelm Röpke, *Against the Tide* (Chicago: H. Regnery, 1969).

42. Ricardo Soares de Oliveira, *Magnificent and Beggar Land: Angola since the Civil War* (New York: Oxford University Press, 2015), 91.

43. Richard McGregor, *The Party: The Secret World of China's Communist Rulers* (New York: Harper, 2010), 14–15.

44. David L. Shambaugh, *China's Future* (New York: Polity, 2016), chap. 4.

45. Generally, see: Terry Lynn Karl, *The Paradox of Plenty: Oil Booms and Petro-States* (Berkeley: University of California Press, 1997).

46. R. A. Hasson, "Rhodesia: A 'Police State'?," *World Today* 22, no. 5 (1966): 181–190, 181–182.

47. Generally, see: Arthur K. Rogers, "The Formulas for State Action," *International Journal of Ethics* 26, no. 3 (1916): 323–338; Herbert Croly, *The Promise of American Life* (New York: Macmillan, 1909).

48. Robert I. Rotberg and Christopher K. Clague, *Haiti: The Politics of Squalor* (Boston: Houghton Mifflin, 1971), 342.

49. Larry Diamond, "The Democratic Rollback: The Resurgence of the Predatory State," *Foreign Affairs* 87, no. 2 (2008): 36–48, 43.

50. For discussion of the emergence of a U.S. regulatory state in the Progressive Era, see: James E. Anderson, *The Emergence of the Modern Regulatory State* (Washington, DC: Public Affairs Press, 1962); Marc T. Law and Sukoo Kim, "The rise of the American regulatory state," in *Handbook on the Politics of Regulation,* D. Levi-Faur, ed. (Cheltenham, UK: Edward Elgar, 2011), 113–128.

51. Generally, see: Cass R. Sunstein, *After the Rights Revolution: Reconceiving the Regulatory State* (Cambridge, MA: Harvard University Press, 1990); Marc Allen Eisner, *Regulatory Politics in Transition* (Baltimore: Johns Hopkins University Press, 2006).

52. Generally, see: Giandomenico Majone, "The Rise of the Regulatory State in Europe," *West European Politics* 17, no. 3 (1994): 77–101; Giandomenico Majone, *Regulating*

Europe (New York: Routledge, 1996); Giandomenico Majone, "From the Positive to the Regulatory State: Causes and Consequences of Changes in the Mode of Governance," *Journal of Public Policy* 17, no. 2 (1997): 139–167.

53. Generally, see: Michael T. Klare, *Rogue States and Nuclear Outlaws: America's Search for a New Foreign Policy* (New York: Hill & Wang, 1995).

54. Generally, see: T. D. Allman, *Rogue State: America at War with the World* (New York: Nation, 2004).

55. Generally, see: Michael Freeman, *Freedom or Security: The Consequences for Democracies Using Emergency Powers to Fight Terror* (Westport, CT: Praeger, 2003); Giorgio Agamben, *State of Exception* (Chicago: University of Chicago Press, 2005).

56. Arend Lijphart, "Emergency Powers and Emergency Regimes: A Commentary," *Asian Survey* 18, no. 4 (1978): 401–407.

57. David C. Unger, *The Emergency State: America's Pursuit of Absolute Security at All Costs* (New York: Penguin, 2012), 1–2 and 281.

58. Suzanne Mettler, *The Submerged State: How Invisible Government Policies Undermine American Democracy* (Chicago: University of Chicago Press, 2011), 4–5.

59. Generally, see: Brian Balogh, *A Government out of Sight: The Mystery of National Authority in Nineteenth-Century America* (New York: Cambridge University Press, 2009).

60. Stephen Spencer, "Architect of the Welfare State," *Church Times,* October 24, 2014; Ernest L. Bogart, "The Changing Economic Functions of Government," *Annals of the American Academy of Political and Social Science* 206 (1939): 1–5, 1.

61. Leo Wolman, "The Beveridge Report," *Political Science Quarterly* 58, no. 1 (1943): 1–10; Charles E. Merriam, "The National Resources Planning Board: A Chapter in American Planning Experience," *American Political Science Review* 38, no. 6 (1944): 1075–1088.

62. The first usage in this sense appears to be from George Stambuk, "Foreign Policy and the Stationing of American Forces Abroad," *Journal of Politics* 25, no. 3 (1963): 472–488, 475.

63. Friedrich Kohlrausch, *A History of Germany* (London: Chapman & Hall, 1844), 506.

64. Derek Croxton, "The Peace of Westphalia of 1648 and the Origins of Sovereignty," *International History Review* 21, no. 3 (1999): 569.

65. Generally, see: Andrew Linklater, "Citizenship and Sovereignty in the Post-Westphalian State," *European Journal of International Relations* 2, no. 1 (1996): 77–103; Andrew Linklater, *Critical Theory and World Politics: Citizenship, Sovereignty and Humanity* (New York: Routledge, 2007).

Index

adaptation, institutional, 8–9, 18, 24–25, 59, 61–64, 69–70, 81, 173n15
administration, institutional, 17–18, 24, 59, 61, 75
administrative states, 46, 141–42
Afghanistan, 8
Albright, Madeleine, 10
American political development (APD), 82–83, 87, 125, 177n4, 185n13
American Revolution, 100
Armitage, David, 82
Australia, 100
authoritarian rule, 5, 35, 44, 68, 72, 109–10, 138–39, 147

Bacon, Francis, 78, 110
Bagehot, Walter, 57
Balogh, Brian, 150
Beard, Charles, 84–85
Beveridge Report, 150
Bismarck, Otto von, 120
Blair, Tony, 136
Bodin, Jean, 78
Botero, Giovanni, 41
Brand, Hal, 48
Brandeis, Louis, 102
Brazil, 88, 100, 144
Britain, 57, 78, 88, 95, 104, 106, 144, 150, 179n4
Brownlow, Louis, 133–34
Bureau of Labor Statistics, 99
Burnham, James, 142
Bush, George W., 44, 74, 76, 101
Butterfield, Herbert, 32, 85–86

Caiden, Gerald, 12
Caldwell, Lynton, 51, 83
Campbell, John, 27
Canada, 68, 88, 144
capitalism, 43, 82, 117, 145
Castells, Manuel, 146–47
censuses, 74, 99
Cerny, Philip, 146

Index

Cheung, Anthony, 12
Chicago, University of, 4, 51
China, 3, 11, 13, 31, 35, 37, 44–45, 67–68, 71, 88–89, 104, 106, 109–10, 132–33, 136, 139, 142, 148, 161n52, 169n10
Christianity, 33
city-states, 3, 32–34, 77, 142
civil liberties, 40, 46, 65–68, 100–101, 148–49
civilian states, 142
civilization states, 89, 142
Clausewitz, Carl von, 67–68
climate change, 8, 41–42, 52, 79, 82, 89, 106, 108–10, 138
Clinton, Bill, 44, 136–37
Clinton, Hillary, 136
Cold War, 5, 62, 85, 105
Columbia University, 129, 187n10
commitment devices, 112–15
communism, 5, 35, 44–45, 68, 138, 148
competition states, 146
conscription, 66
consolidation, institutional, 14, 17–18, 24–25, 38, 59–61, 63–64, 70, 79
Croly, Herbert, 148

Dahl, Robert, 51
de Tocqueville, Alexis, 104, 114
deep states, 143
Democratic Party, 44, 136
Department of Defense, 108, 188n7
Department of Foreign Affairs, 33
Department of State, 33, 96, 188n7
design, institutional, 17–18, 24, 38, 59–61, 70, 81, 107, 112
developmental states, 11, 46, 141, 143
Dewey, John, 61, 132
Diamond, Larry, 148–49
Dimock, Marshall, 27, 37
Durant, Robert, 8
Duranty, Walter, 117

Earle, Edward Mead, 47
Ecevit, Bülent, 143
economic regulation, 7–8, 11, 30, 44, 53, 66, 99–101, 133, 149
efficiency, 6–7, 10, 15, 93–97, 125, 138
Eisenhower, Dwight, 145
Eisenhower Executive Office Building, 96
Embargo Act, 75–76

emergency states, 149–50
empires, 32–33, 143–44
Environmental Protection Agency, 99
European Union, 147
exceptionalism, 87–89

failed states, 78–79, 144
fascism, 5, 117, 138, 148
Federal Reserve, 115
financial crisis of 2007/2008, 69, 82, 85, 101, 105, 136
Finer, S. E., 28–29
fiscal-military states, 46, 144
Florence, 3, 32, 34, 77–78
fragile states, 13–15, 27, 41, 60, 78, 88, 95, 99, 141, 144, 163n67, 167n10
Fragile States Index, 15, 163n72
France, 88, 179n4
Fraser Institute, 100
free markets, 10, 43, 45–46, 88, 98–101, 133, 145
Freedom House, 100
Friedman, Thomas, 113
frontier states, 88, 141, 144–45
Fukuyama, Francis, 9–10, 63
Fund for Peace, 15, 163n72

Gaddis, John Lewis, 47
Galbraith, J. K., 142
Galson, William, 9
Gandhi, Mahatma, 37
garrison states, 8, 46, 142, 145
Gaus, John, 5, 51
Georgetown University, 129, 187n9
Georgia, University of, 186n5
Germany, 88, 117, 120, 138, 147, 150, 179n4
Giddens, Anthony, 26
Global Forum on Reinventing Government, 10, 160n41
Goodnow, Frank, 57–58
Gore, Al, 10
grand strategy concept, 47–49, 169n11
Great Depression, 54, 96, 101, 105, 117, 137
Greece, 84, 95, 142
Grimmelikhuijsen, Stephan, 17
Guldi, Jo, 82
Gulick, Luther, 4, 51

Hall, John, 27
Haque, Shamsul, 11

Hardt, Michael, 144
Hasson, R. A., 148
Hastings, Adrian, 146
Hay, Colin, 26
healthcare, 6–7, 11, 70, 84, 97, 100, 150
historical institutionalism (HI), 173n1, 177n4
Ho, Alfred Tat-Kei, 12
Hobbes, Thomas, 32–33, 77
hollow states, 145
Hughes, Owen, 7
human rights, 3, 40–41, 46, 65–67, 88, 99–101, 103, 106, 111, 167n16
Hungary, 139
Huntington, Samuel, 56, 58, 106

Ignatieff, Michael, 106
Ikenberry, John, 27
Im, Tobin, 12–13
immigration, 4, 66–67, 105–6
India, 11, 88–89, 95, 110, 132, 142, 161n52, 161n55
Indonesia, 88
intelligence gathering, 7, 36, 39, 77, 117, 143
internal order, 2, 5, 38, 65–68, 78, 95, 103–6, 111, 117, 136, 138–39, 148
International Monetary Fund, 10, 108, 163n67
Iraq, 8, 149
Ireland, 105, 179n4
Israel, 31, 170n24
Italy, 32, 88, 117, 138, 142, 168n19, 179n4

James, William, 118
Japan, 11, 104, 143, 146
Jefferson, Thomas, 61, 75, 104, 110, 119, 181n1
Jilke, Sebastian, 17
Johns Hopkins University, 129, 187n8
Johnson, Chalmers, 143
Johnson, Lyndon, 76, 118
Johnson, Paul, 57
journals, 6, 11, 126, 137, 139, 163n65, 163n69

Kahn, Alfred, 118
Katznelson, Ira, 87
Kennan, George, 173n16
Kennedy, Paul, 47, 170n17
Kettl, Donald, 8–9, 80
Kim Jong-un, 36
Kissinger, Henry, 67, 170n24
Kosovo, 31
Krugman, Paul, 78–79

laissez-faire economic policy, 67, 136, 147–49
Lasswell, Harold, 142, 145
law of unintended consequences, 119–20, 184n14
legitimacy, 11, 14, 23–24, 27–28, 34, 39–40, 94, 97, 102, 109, 111, 119, 125, 138, 147, 165n15
Lenin, Vladimir, 148
Leviathan, 33
Libya, 149
Liddell Hart, B. H., 47
Lijphart, Arend, 149–50
Lippmann, Walter, 4, 73, 117, 138
Lister, Michael, 26
Lofgren, Mike, 143
Los Angeles, 95
Luttwak, Edward, 48

Machiavelli, Niccolò, 3, 32, 34, 68, 77–78, 84, 142
MacIver, R. M., 61–62
Mahoney, James, 56
managerial states, 142
Manchester school of economic liberalism, 147
Mao Zedong, 46
March, James, 56, 62
market states, 145–46
Marx, Karl, 69, 129, 175n10
Maxwell School (Syracuse University), 186n5
McCarthy, Joseph, 106
megatrends, 8, 159n27, 160n28
Merriam, Charles, 5, 15, 38, 79, 116, 118, 176n14
Mettler, Suzanne, 96, 150
Mexico, 104, 106
military-industrial complex, 45–46, 145
Mill, John Stuart, 146, 166n20
Miller, Peter, 83
Milward, Brint, 8
Ministry of International Trade and Industry (MITI), 143
Monaco, 142
Monroe Doctrine, 104
multinational states, 30, 146
Mussolini, Benito, 117

National Academy of Public Administration (NAPA), 135–37
National Resources Planning Board, 150
national security, 5, 7–8, 38, 53, 59, 66–67, 77, 108, 113, 136, 138–39, 145

Index

national security states, 8, 145
nation-states, 29, 99, 144, 146–47, 166n20
nativism, 105–6
Negri, Antonio, 144
neoliberal states, 146
network states, 146–47
new public management (NPM), 10–12, 160n39
night-watchmen states, 46, 147
Nixon, Richard, 76
North, Douglass, 56
North Korea, 31, 36, 149

Obama, Barack, 41–42
Occupational Safety and Health Administration, 99
oil, 32, 45, 105, 108–9, 148
Okimoto, Daniel, 146
Okrent, David, 75–76
Olsen, Asmus Leth, 17
Olsen, Johan, 56, 62
Olson, Mancur, 63
Orbán, Viktor, 139
ordoliberal states, 147

Palestine, 31
Pande, Aparna, 89
pandemics, 54, 82
Paris Accord, 41
party states, 147–48
Peace of Westphalia, 32, 150–51
petro-states, 46, 148
Philippines, 104
Plato, 84
police states, 148
policing, 2, 6, 11, 39, 95, 97–98, 105, 148
Pollitt, Christopher, 8, 83, 160n
Popular Movement for the Liberation of Angola (MPLA), 147–48
positive states, 148
poverty, 2, 76, 118, 144
Powell, Colin, 94
Powell Doctrine, 94
predatory states, 148–49
presentism, 82–86
Prince, The, 32, 68, 142
prisons, 9, 12
progressive movement, 4–5, 9, 15, 72–73, 94, 101, 118, 171n1

Prohibition, 75–76
protected states, 149
protests, 1, 34, 66–68, 95, 109, 146
public management approach, 6–16, 19, 124–26, 158n15, 159n19
Putin, Vladimir, 45, 57

Qatar, 142

Raadschelders, Jos, 83
raison d'état thinking, 41–42, 71, 89
Rauch, Jonathan, 63
Reagan, Ronald, 44, 69, 136–37
realism, 38, 77–80, 176n14
rebellions, 14, 34, 66, 78, 94–95
regulatory states, 7, 19, 46, 128, 149
Republican Party, 44, 136
rogue states, 149
Roosevelt, Franklin, 70, 79, 101, 116–17, 120
Rosenbloom, David, 8
Russia, 36–37, 45–46, 57, 72, 88–89, 144

Sanders, Bernie, 136
Saudi Arabia, 100
Schlesinger, Arthur, 83
School of Advanced International Studies (Johns Hopkins), 129, 187n8
School of Foreign Service (Georgetown University), 129, 187n9
Schumpeter, Joseph, 70
secessionist movements, 29, 34, 75, 101
September 11 terrorist attacks, 66, 74, 149
Serbia, 31
Sheehan, James, 142
shock and awe, 95
Singapore, 142
Sisk, Timothy, 60
Skocpol, Theda, 28
social forces, 52, 84, 171n9
social programs, 5–8, 16, 44, 86, 118–19
South Korea, 12–13, 31, 143
Southern California, University of, 186n5
Soviet Union, 5, 10, 14, 32, 36, 45–46, 57, 67, 117, 138, 144, 148
Spanish-American War, 144
Spencer, Stephen, 150
Spruyt, Hendrick, 82
Spykman, Nicolas, 62